W9-CHZ-568

Tiger Cub

by Monica Hughes

Consultant: Mitch Cronick

BEARPORT
PUBLISHING COMPANY, INC.
New York, New York

Credits

t=top, b=bottom, c=center, l=left, r=right, OFC=outside front cover
Alamy: 13, 22bl. Corbis: 4, 5, 6t, 19, 20, 21. FLPA: OFC, 1, 6b, 11.
Getty: 14. Photolibrary (Oxford Scientific): 12, 15. Superstock: 7, 8–9, 16–17, 18, 22c.

Library of Congress Cataloging-in-Publication Data

Hughes, Monica.
Tiger cub / by Monica Hughes.
p. cm. — (I love reading)
Includes bibliographical references and index.
ISBN 1-59716-155-1 (library binding) — ISBN 1-59716-181-0 (pbk.)
1. Tiger cubs — Juvenile literature. I. Title. II. Series.

QL737.C23H85 2006
599.756'139 — dc22

2005029868

For more information, write to Bearport Publishing Company, Inc., 101 Fifth Avenue, Suite 6R, New York, New York 10003.
Printed in the United States of America.

1 2 3 4 5 6 7 8 9 10

The I Love Reading series was originally developed by Tick Tock Media.

CONTENTS

What is a tiger? 4

What do tigers look like? 6

Meet a tiger cub 8

When does a tiger cub open his eyes? 10

How does a mother care for her cubs? 12

What does a tiger cub eat? 14

How does a tiger cub learn to hunt? 16

When does a tiger cub live on his own? 18

Why are tigers in danger? 20

Glossary 22

Index 24

Learn More 24

What is a tiger?

A tiger is a big, wild cat.

Tigers live in the forests and **jungles** of **Asia**.

Tiger

Here are some other big cats.

What do tigers look like?

Tigers have orange and white fur with black stripes.

They have big teeth.

They have sharp claws.

Some tigers are white with blue eyes.

Meet a tiger cub

This is a tiger cub with his mother.

There are two cubs in the **litter**.

The tiger cubs are born **blind**.

Mother tiger

When does a tiger cub open his eyes?

The tiger cub opens his eyes after two weeks.

His eyes are blue.

They will turn yellow when he gets older.

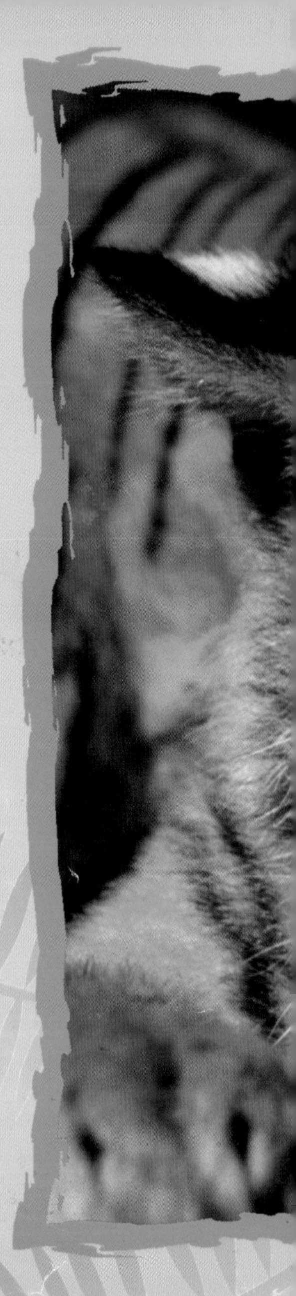

How does a mother care for her cubs?

The mother keeps the cubs in a **den**.

She washes them with her tongue.

She carries the cubs in her mouth.

What does a tiger cub eat?

The tiger cub drinks his mother's milk.

After six months, he can eat meat.

So his mother catches
small animals for him.

How does a tiger cub learn to hunt?

The mother tiger takes the cubs hunting.

They watch her jump on her **prey**.

The cubs play and jump on each other.

When does a tiger cub live on his own?

After two years, the tiger cub will live on his own.

He marks his part of the forest by scratching trees.

He roars if another tiger comes by.

Why are tigers in danger?

First, many tigers are killed for their fur.

Second, the forests and jungles where tigers live are in danger.

The trees are cut down so houses and farms can be built.

Without trees, there are fewer places for tigers to live.

Glossary

Asia (AY-zhuh) a part of the world where wild tigers live

blind (BLINDE) not able to see

den (DEN) the home of a wild animal in a cave or hollow tree

jungles (JUHNG-guhlz) thick forests in hot places

litter (LIT-ur) a group of animals born at the same time

prey (PRAY) an animal that is hunted for food

Index

Asia 4
big cats 4–5
cheetah 5
claws 6
cubs 8–9, 10–11, 12–13, 14–15, 16–17, 18–19
dangers to tigers 20–21
den 12
eyes 7, 10
food 14–15
forests 4, 18, 20
fur 6, 20
hunting 16–17
jungles 4, 20
leopard 5
lion 5
mother tigers 8–9, 12–13, 14–15, 16
playing 17
teeth 6

Learn More

Hewett, Joan. *A Tiger Cub Grows Up.* Minneapolis, MN: Lerner Publishing Group (2001).

Thomson, Sarah L. *Tigers.* New York: HarperCollins (2004).

www.animaland.org/asp/encyclopedia/tiger.asp

www.savethetigerfund.org/Directory/kids.htm

Johnsgard, Paul A.
Dragons and unicorns.

UTICA PUBLIC LIBRARY
UTICA, MICHIGAN
Presented by
CITY OF UTICA
EMPLOYEES
In Memory of
MURRAY V. WILLSON

DRAGONS AND UNICORNS

A Natural History

Paul and Karin Johnsgard

ST. MARTIN'S PRESS / NEW YORK

 For information, address St. Martin's Press, 175 Fifth Avenue, New York, N.Y. 10010.

Design by Laura Hammond

Library of Congress Cataloging in Publication Data

Johnsgard, Paul A.
Dragons and unicorns.

1. Dragons. 2. Unicorns. I. Johnsgard, Karin. II. Title.
GR830.D7J63 398. 2'454 82-5630
ISBN 0-312-21895-8 AACR2

First Edition
10 9 8 7 6 5 4 3 2 1

For those who still look
for cloven hoofprints in mountain meadows,
and for smoke clouds
rising from the mouths of caves

CONTENTS

PREFACE xi

INTRODUCTION xiii

I. DRAGONS 1

A Classification of Dragons 1

Evolution and Anatomy 3

The Kinds of Living Dragons 12

The European Fire-Breathing Dragon 12, *The Oriental Mist-Breathing Dragon* 14, *The American Flightless Dragon* 19, *Flying Dragons* 20, *Lake Dragons* 21

LIFE HISTORIES 23

Flight and Migration 23, *Foods and General Behavior* 26, *Special Senses* 31, *Breathing of Fire and Mist* 33, *Enemies* 35, *Reproduction and Longevity* 36, *Social Organization and Justice* 42

II. DRAGONS AND MAN 46

The Dragons of Antiquity 46

Dragon Slayers of Medieval Times 51
Dragons of the Late Middle Ages and Renaissance 55
Recent Dragon Sightings 59
Myths and Misconceptions 61
Treasure Hoarding 61, *Child Stealing* 63, *Medicinal Uses of Dragon Parts* 66
Protection and Conservation 69
Current Controversies about Origins 75

III. UNICORNS 79
The Evolution of Unicorns 79
Modern Species of Unicorns 84
Life Histories 88
Anatomy 89, *Locomotion* 91, *Reproduction* 92, *Daily Life* 96, *Adult Life and Old Age* 100

IV. UNICORNS AND MAN 103
Unicorns of the Ancient World 104
The Medieval Unicorn 121
The Preservation of Unicorns 132

V. SOME FINAL THOUGHTS 135

COMPLETE CHECKLIST AND FIELD-IDENTIFICATION GUIDE TO DRAGONS AND UNICORNS 138

ADDITIONAL INFORMATION FOR DRAGON AND UNICORN WATCHERS 151

GLOSSARY 154

BIBLIOGRAPHY 161

PREFACE

As most people now know, our dragon and unicorn populations have declined precipitously in recent years. Not only have dragons been excluded from all "nice" neighborhoods and driven out of most states, but they are hated almost everywhere, in spite of the fact that they are now protected by federal law. Unicorns too are on the verge of extinction, though for different reasons. Unicorns have suffered primarily from our unwillingness to leave enough wilderness and opportunities for personal freedom as are necessary for such an innocent and solitary animal to survive. Nor have we adequately prevented exploitation of unicorns by those who capture them for exhibition in carnivals and circuses or cut off their magical horns for personal profit.

Because most people are woefully ignorant of the importance of both dragons and unicorns in maintaining stable worldwide ecosystems, and of the values inherent in protecting the faunal diversity represented by dragons and unicorns, we are offering this summary of the natural histories of these great beasts. In the news media, an increasing public intolerance of dragons is in evidence, and the capture of unicorns has once again become an irresistible temptation for many. It is hoped that after reading this book the reader will join in a grass-roots movement to ensure the basic rights of dragons and allow them, no matter how different their appearance and culture from ours, to live out their lives in peace. We hope as well that people will learn to respect the privacy of unicorns and willingly offer them the open spaces and clean environment they need for survival, without expecting anything more in return than the simple pleasure of knowing that they are content in their chosen solitude. Finally, although unicorns have little reason to believe in us, the least *we* can do is to believe in them.

—P.A.J. and K.L.J.

INTRODUCTION

For some centuries now, humans have generally believed that the last dragon died in medieval times, perhaps at the hands of an overzealous knight determined to add a dangerous serpent to his life-list of victories over evil, or that the species became extinct because most pre-Flood dragons were excluded from Noah's ark, owing to their bad breath and tendencies to set things on fire. The unicorn was one of the first animals to be shifted from the Middle Ages list of huntable species to the category of "declining and in danger of extinction," thanks to habitat destruction and the selfish human demand for their precious horns.

It is our intention here to review the life histories of these great beasts, to try to learn if any of them might still exist, and, if so, to suggest a strategy for preserving the last remaining populations from extinction. In doing so, we will make judgments and offer hypotheses that, to some, may place the book somewhere between fact and fantasy, but we hope that the reader will bear with us, for to doubt the existence of dragons and unicorns is surely the hallmark of a limited imagination and a closed mind.

In preparing this book we have had to review many old references and have sometimes relied on accounts that were written before photography or other means of scientific verification were possible. A number of these early accounts had to be translated from obscure languages. Furthermore, both dragons and unicorns have traditionally suffered from "bad press," inasmuch as dragons have all too often been blamed for such diverse catastrophes as crop failures, earthquakes, hurricanes, and volcanic eruptions, when in fact they were probably feeding peacefully in the woods at the time. Likewise, the unicorn's horn has been so coveted that people have invented any number of untrue and malicious stories about the beast in order to justify its capture or killing. It is through this tangled maze of deceptions and half-truths that we must make our way, to try to get at the truth about dragons, unicorns, and their kin and to understand their unusual lives.

INTRODUCTION

The question of historicity and actuality with regard to gods and unicorns is a relatively trifling matter which may be left to antiquarians and biologists, for both the god and the unicorn had a business to perform greater than any mere existence in the flesh could explain or provide a basis for.

Odell Shepard, *The Lore of the Unicorn*

I. DRAGONS

Among all the kindes of serpents, there is none comparable to the dragon.

Edward Topsell, 1658

A Classification of Dragons

Much of the confusion about dragons has resulted from the fact that several kinds have existed in the past and that early observers failed to distinguish among dragons, snakes, and other reptiles. Nearly all of these were simply referred to as "worms" or "serpents" and were probably greatly shunned; few people would have lingered long enough near such an animal to count its legs or toes and try to classify it. We can classify now all these reptiles quite simply as snakes if they have no external legs, as lizards if they are relatively small (usually smaller than a bread box) and have four legs, and as dragons if they are considerably larger, with four legs or with two legs and two wings. Of course, many well-meaning artists draw typical dragons as having four legs and two wings, but that is obviously impossible. The origin of the wings of dragons has been from their forelegs, as in birds, bats, and other flying reptiles. Beyond the question of the number of legs, it is clear that several different species of dragons evolved, depending on their needs for swimming or flying. The major types include:

1. Lake dragons: Creatures whose legs have been converted into paddles and who are unable to leave water. These include such types as the Loch Ness "monster," and related forms found in the lakes of Canada and the United States.
2. Flying dragons: Small reptiles that have converted their forelegs into wings. These include one modern species in which both sexes can fly, as well as some fossil types in which apparently only the smaller male was able to fly, while the heavier female was flightless. Not to be confused with similar flying reptiles, the pterosaurs.
3. Flightless dragons: These are the largest kinds of dragons, and those most frequently vilified. Most are depicted as fire-breathing, carnivorous monsters, but in fact all of them are primarily vegetarians, and none is actually able to breathe

fire. However, all species generate flammable gas, and the European dragon is able to ignite this gas when it is threatened.

Before going further, we must consider the word "dragon" itself. It is derived from the Greek word *drakon*. This perhaps in turn may have come from *derkomai*, to look terrible or to gleam. The word "dragon" has itself given rise to "dragoon," a type of musket-armed British cavalry soldier, whose frightful appearance during a charge probably reminded the populace (or the opposing army) of fire-breathing dragons. Similarly, the Romans used the *draco*, a wind-socklike flag in the shape of a flying dragon, to signify the approach of a group of about five hundred men, which must also have thrown fear into the hearts of their enemies. Even the Vikings used dragonlike figureheads to decorate the prows of their ships. In the fifteenth century a war machine in the form of a dragon, with a cannon protruding from the mouth or stomach, was designed for use in Arabia. No wonder so many people fear dragons—or at least their human counterparts!

Evolution and Anatomy

Since no modern zoologist has yet been able to capture a living dragon, or even obtain a freshly killed specimen, we must rely on the evidence provided by fossil dinosaurs and dragons to get an idea of their internal anatomy and other structures.

As is well known, the Age of Reptiles, which ended less than one hundred million years ago, was a period when hundreds of species of dragonlike creatures stalked the earth. Among the largest and most dangerous were the meat-eating dinosaurs, such as *Tyrannosaurus* and *Allosaurus,* which terrorized all the smaller reptiles. Surprisingly, these large and ponderous beasts, although they ruled the land surfaces of the earth, were not the ancestors of the modern-day dragons. This we can know from the fact that all the meat-eating dinosaurs belonged to a group called lizard-hipped reptiles, whose heavy hip-bone structure was very different from the birdlike hips of the ancestors of our present-day dragons. Carnivorous dinosaurs also lack the special bone at the tip of the lower jaw that all real dragons have, which serves as a beaklike device for clipping vegetation. A dragon's teeth are small and sharp, designed basically for chewing plants. The bird-hipped dinosaurs were often much smaller than the lizard-hipped ones, with slender bodies and long hind legs that allowed them to run very fast. Their forelegs were modified for holding food and, as we shall see, were later converted into winglike structures.

It is obvious that the small wings of these early dragons could not possibly have allowed the animals to take off and instead probably served only as display structures that the animal might have spread to make it seem more ferocious when confronted with a meat-eating dinosaur. With time, the wings grew progressively larger and more useful for short, gliding flights; they evolved to allow true flight in the smaller species. The larger dragons, however, had little or no need to escape through flight. They retained only small wings or, in some cases, never evolved wings at all, at least among the females.

Apart from the wings, the skeletons of early dragons such as *Protodraco** of the late Mesozoic very closely resembled those of such contemporary dinosaurs as *Hypsilophodon*. They were about five feet long, weighed about one hundred fifty pounds, and had a long tail that provided a counterbalance when they ran. Males of *Protodraco* had eleven pairs of ribs (females had ten), and in both sexes the teeth were small and ridged for crushing foods. *Protodraco*'s wings were about three feet long.

*Paleontologists searching for details on *Protodraco* and its relatives should look for it alphabetically, immediately following the Piltdown man.

Protodraco apparently lived for several million years but was eventually replaced by a more advanced type, *Mesodraco,* near the end of the Mesozoic Era. In *Mesodraco,* the forelegs were more fully developed into winglike structures, and the hind legs and tail had become smaller, as the center of gravity of the animal had to be shifted forward and the weight reduced for taking off. There is some doubt about whether *Mesodraco* could fly very well; instead it probably just climbed up high cliffs and jumped off to glide downward. It was about ten feet long, with wings about six feet long, and it weighed several hundred pounds.

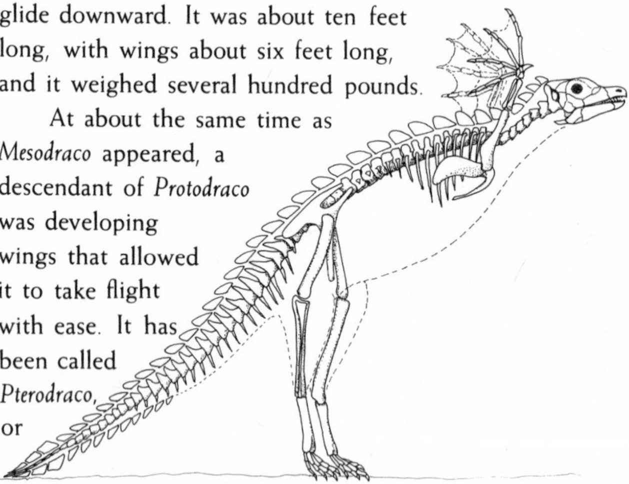

At about the same time as *Mesodraco* appeared, a descendant of *Protodraco* was developing wings that allowed it to take flight with ease. It has been called *Pterodraco,* or "winged dragon." Unlike the pterosaurs of the same period, its wings were supported by four bony fingers rather than one, and thus it was able to fly with a heavier load. It captured some of the primitive birds that were just then developing flight and sometimes ate young pterosaurs, perhaps hastening their extinction. It gradually gave up vegetation as a major food, and turned instead to eating meat. There were probably several species of *Pterodraco*; a few fossil remains suggest that the largest species may have had a wingspread of up to forty feet and weighed several hundred pounds. They must indeed have been terrifying monsters, but these large species of flying dragon gradually disappeared. The only species living today *(Pterodraco volans)* is about five feet long, with a wingspread of up to ten feet, and weighs about forty pounds. That still makes it as heavy as the heaviest flying bird now known.

Early in the Age of Mammals, the Cenozoic Era, *Mesodraco* evidently died out and was replaced by the modern form of dragon, *Neodraco*. This dragon type is still larger than *Mesodraco* and is totally flightless, even in males. Three species of *Neodraco* exist: the American flightless dragon (*Neodraco americana*), the European fire-breathing dragon (*Neodraco pyrogena*), and the Oriental or mist-breathing dragon (*Neodraco pluvialis*). They probably all evolved from the earlier *Mesodraco* type, and all have several characteristics in common. One such feature is that all are basically vegetarians, their teeth designed for clipping vegetation. The European dragon, however, has modified its stomach in such a way as to divide it into three separate compartments. The first of these is for rapid digestion of starches and sugar-rich foods, which provide quick energy. The second is a large compartment for the temporary storage and digestion of cellulose and other woodlike materials that can only be digested by bacteria through fermentation. In the course of such fermentation, the material releases much methane gas, which is stored in the third stomach compartment. Whenever the animal so desires, it can belch this or another stomach gas, producing a vile smell that tends to frighten away other creatures. If this is not sufficient to scare off an intruder, the animal quickly gnashes its teeth together so violently that sparks fly, igniting the gas and producing the fire-breathing effect so feared by man.

Although the American and Oriental dragons also produce methane gas through similar digestive methods, their stomachs lack the third compartment, and they more or less continuously release the gas in a misty stream. They are therefore not able to store up enough to produce the overwhelming effects of the European dragon, and they are also unable to ignite the

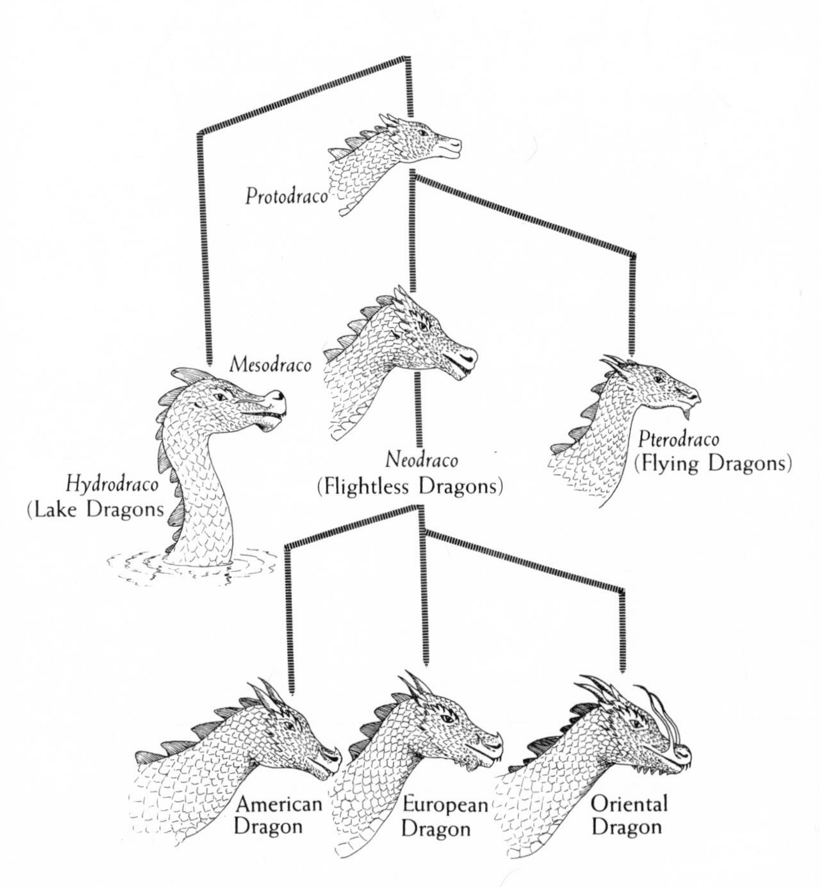
Protodraco
Mesodraco
Hydrodraco
(Lake Dragons
Neodraco
(Flightless Dragons)
Pterodraco
(Flying Dragons)
American
Dragon
European
Dragon
Oriental
Dragon

limited amounts of methane that are released during normal breathing. Yet, over time, a great deal of methane is nevertheless generated, and the misty clouds that constantly rise from a dragon's lair are among the best clues in tracking them down. (One must, of course, avoid striking matches on such a search.) However, even full-grown dragons are able to conceal themselves behind a misty smoke screen that they exhale when caught well away from their lairs; this is another reason that they are so rarely seen by humans.

Although these dragons are essentially vegetarians, they will sometimes capture and eat small birds just for the exercise, and all of them are dangerous when cornered by other animals and humans. This is especially true of the fire-breathing European dragon, as many knights learned too late. But dragons are mostly active at night; their eyes cannot withstand bright sunlight. It is generally safe to walk past dragon weyrs on sunny days.

The last major type of dragon, the lake dragons, have had a rather different evolutionary history, and perhaps should not be called dragons at all. They evolved from a separate ancestral plesiosaur (swimming reptile) stock, also during the Mesozoic Era, and their internal anatomy is not at all like that of the

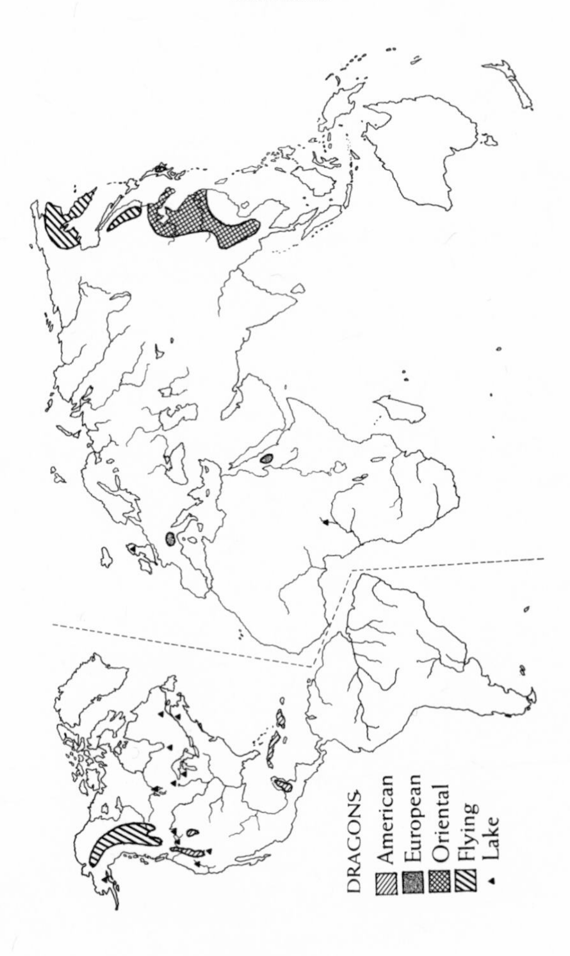
DRAGONS
American
European
Oriental
Flying
Lake

dragon types already mentioned. Their legs have no traces of separate toes, but instead have been converted into long and flattened flipperlike structures, and their tails have developed into a vertical fin. Because they eat fish, their stomachs have never been modified for cellulose digestion, and they therefore do not breathe methane. Also, unlike the land dragons, all of which lay eggs that develop outside their bodies, the young of the lake dragons are born alive in the water. Therefore, unlike egg-laying turtles and crocodiles, they need never emerge on land at all and so are rarely observed outside the water. Almost nobody has ever had a full view of a lake dragon; most drawings are based on imagination or only limited views. Nevertheless, we can be sure that the animals looked much like the ancient plesiosaurs from which they evolved and do not bear much resemblance to other dragon types.

The Kinds of Living Dragons

Dragons beget dragons, and phoenixes beget phoenixes.
Chinese Proverb

THE EUROPEAN FIRE-BREATHING DRAGON

Dragons have lived in Europe for countless ages. Leviathan, the giant creature mentioned in the Book of

Job, with a burning gaze, a fire-breathing mouth, and scales so thick that it was immune to weapons, was certainly a typical dragon. Unfortunately, early Christians came to confuse the real peace-loving dragons with serpentlike symbols of evil. They even began to believe that it was a dragon that had offered Eve the apple and had thus helped bring about man's expulsion from Paradise. Because of this, dragons fell out of favor very early in western history, and few people had anything nice to say about them. Most descriptions of dragons by Europeans are strongly flavored by such biases, and it is hard indeed to find a credible account.

As best we can judge by both the earlier descriptions and fairly recent sightings, the European dragon is at least sixty feet long as an adult. Some specimens may occasionally reach even greater lengths, since dragons, like snakes and other reptiles, continue to grow throughout their lifetimes. The European dragon has very large hind legs and feet; the hind feet are strong and powerful, with three clawed toes in front, and a smaller fourth toe facing inward. The front legs are smaller and in the male take the shape of rudimentary wings. There is a long tail capable of being coiled up. The head is large, with a long snout and forked tongue. The jaws are equipped with many sharply pointed teeth, all about the same size. The two large eyes are especially well equipped for seeing in the semidarkness of caves and mountain recesses. Between the two eyes is a third eyelike structure called the "dracontia," once believed to be a precious gem with many magical powers. Most of the dragon's body is covered by small, greenish scales, which blend in with vegetation for camouflage; on the underside is a group of bright yellow scales, even brighter in females. A series of sharp protective spines extends down the back, from the crown to the end of the tail. The rudimentary wings of the male probably also serve a protective function—to direct a stream of fire toward enemies or, when spread and waved, with their brilliant colors exposed, to present an effective threat display. In females the forelegs have the usual shape, and the feet and claws are well adapted for digging, in conjunction with their egg-laying behavior.

THE ORIENTAL MIST-BREATHING DRAGON

In contrast to the European dragon, Oriental dragons rarely, if ever, breathe fire but do breathe heavy mists and can often produce rain clouds. Many of their other characteristics are found in groups of nine, a number that is known to be lucky. For example, typical Chinese dragons have eighty-one scales running down the dorsal ridge of their backs, representing the square of a lucky number. Including a rather primitive dragon (*k'uei*) that can be seen on ancient Chinese bronzes, there are nine major types of Chinese dragons. These include the horned dragon, the winged dragon, the celestial dragon (which supports and protects the mansions of the gods), the spiritual dragon (which generates wind and rain for the benefit of mankind), the dragon of hidden treasures (which keeps guard over concealed wealth), the coiling dragon (which lives in water), and the yellow dragon (which once emerged from water and presented the legendary Emperor Fu Hsi with the elements of writing).* The last of the nine is the dragon king, which actually consists of four separate dragons, each of which rules over one of the four seas, those of the east, south, west, and north.

The most powerful generalized type of Chinese dragon is the horned dragon, or *lung,* which can produce rain and is totally deaf. Additionally, there are a hornless dragon (*li*) that lives in the ocean and another type (*chiao*) that is scale-covered and usually

*See also page 104.

inhabits marshes but also keeps dens in the mountains.

There are also nine ways in which the Chinese have traditionally represented these dragons, each revealing different dragon characteristics. There are dragons carved on the tops of bells and gongs, because of the beast's habit of calling loudly when attacked. A second type is carved on the screws of fiddles, since most dragons are fond of music. A third is carved on the tops of stone tablets, because of dragons' love of literature. A fourth is found at the bottom of stone monuments, as dragons can support heavy weights. A fifth is placed on the eaves of temples, as dragons are ever alert to danger. A sixth occurs on the beams of bridges, since dragons are fond of water. A seventh is carved on Buddha's throne, as dragons like to rest. An eighth is placed on the hilts of swords, since dragons are known to be capable of slaughter. The ninth is carved on prison gates, as these are dragons that are fond of quarreling and troublemaking.

The colors of Chinese dragons are evidently quite variable, but in the case of the *chiao* type its back is striped with green, its sides are yellow, and it is crimson underneath. The nine major characteristics of a *lung*-type dragon include a head like a camel's, horns like a deer's, eyes like a hare's, ears like a bull's, a neck like an iguana's, a belly like a frog's, scales like a carp's, paws like a tiger's, and claws like an eagle's. It has a pair of large canine teeth in its upper jaw. The long, tendril-like whiskers extending from either side of its mouth are probably used for feeling its way along the bottom of muddy ponds. In color it varies from greenish to golden, with a series of alternating short and long spines extending down the back and along the tail, where they become longer.

Unlike the European dragon, Chinese dragons lay only a single egg, which they carry about often beneath the chin, rather than lay a clutch of eggs and incubate them in a dry place. However, in both species the eggs are exceptionally hard and stonelike and may require many months to hatch. The egg in its early stages is usually white and resembles a pearl, but late in incubation it changes to a golden, or even a reddish-gold, hue.

Chinese dragons spend the winter months out of sight, resting in lakes or pools or water, but in spring they are able to rise into the sky on great waterspouts or during volcanic eruptions; thus it is that they are usually associated with thunder, rain, and moisture. Chinese dragons are usually mild-tempered and rarely bother people, but they are extremely fond of small birds, like sparrows and swallows, and are inclined to gulp down any that happen to fly too close to the water's surface. So fond are they of this food that a human who has recently eaten cooked bird meat and walks near water is in danger of being captured and consumed by a hungry dragon!

The Japanese dragons are very close relatives of the Chinese dragons and probably evolved from them. As in China, there are many subtypes of dragons, but typically the Japanese dragon has only three claws per foot, is somewhat more snakelike than its Chinese relative, and always has a bristly row of spines along the back, or even a double row. Japanese dragons are thought to live primarily in rivers and seas. The general Japanese name for dragon is *tatsu,* the equivalent of the Chinese *lung.* Both cultures recognize four dragon kings that rule over the earth and live at its very edges. The four Japanese dragon kings are the *sui riu,* the dragon that produces reddish rain when it is suffering; the *han riu,* a multistriped dragon about forty feet long; the *ka riu,* fiery red but only about seven feet long; and the *ri riu,* able to see for more than one hundred miles. The winged dragon of Japan is the *hai riu,* and the dragon of good luck is the *fuku riu.*

The Japanese believe that a female dragon gives birth to nine young, each of which has a different attribute. (Note the similarities to the attributes assigned to dragons in Chinese culture.) The first likes to sing, and thus Japanese bells have dragonlike tops. The second is fond of music, and the koto and suzumi instruments are decorated with dragons. The third is fond of drinking, and thus drinking vessels are so adorned. The fourth likes dangerous and steep places, so the beams of temples and pagodas are provided with dragons. The fifth is fond of killing and bloodshed, and thus swords are decorated with dragons. The sixth loves learning, and so book covers have dragon decorations. The seventh is noted for its hearing abilities and can be seen on drumheads, gongs, and chimes. The eighth likes to sit, and so chairs have carved dragon ornaments. The ninth likes to bear heavy weights, and thus the legs of tables and hibachi have dragonlike feet.

THE AMERICAN FLIGHTLESS DRAGON

The flightless dragon of America is now mostly confined to part of the Caribbean and Mexico's Yucatan Peninsula, but probably once ranged over most of the North and South American continents. It seems to be more akin to the Oriental mist-breathing dragons than to the European fire-breathing type, since it has never been known to roast any human victims when threatened. However, it has a powerful breath, capable of "seeding" the clouds and stimulating rainfall.

In the Caribbean, it is called *Huracan* and is believed to be responsible for causing hurricanes. On the Yucatan Peninsula, it is called *Kukulcan* or *Chac* and dwells in deep, water-filled limestone caverns, or *cenotes.* It is thought to control the onset of summer rains, and was once greatly worshipped by the Mayans because of its remarkable powers over the weather. In the Caribbean islands there are few freshwater lakes or pools, so it inhabits primarily the open seas, mainly in the triangular area bounded by Bermuda, Puerto Rico, and Florida. The weather there is often plagued by tropical storms during the spring mating season, when the dragons are very active; their activities stimulate so much rainfall that planes and ocean-going vessels lose their way and sometimes disappear.

FLYING DRAGONS

Although the fire-breathing and mist-breathing dragons are believed by many to be able to fly with ease, stories of the larger dragons' flight patterns actually result from confusion with a much smaller species of dragon, which rarely reaches a length of more than about five or ten feet. These smaller dragons are more common in the Orient than in Europe; in China they are called the *ying lung*, or winged dragons, and in Japan they are known as the *hai rivo, tobi tatsu*, or *sachi hoko*. Very few good descriptions of these dragons exist. They fly at night and are very quiet, so they are rarely seen in flight. They have often been confused with eagles or condors. Nor can they be easily seen on the ground. They are remarkable mimics and can change their colors according to their surroundings. Thus, though a dragon on the ground is relatively helpless, it is often almost totally invisible, camouflaged by the rocks or earth around it. In the air, however, these dragons can readily be detected by radar, and thus we can state with certainty that their wingspan is rarely more than ten feet and that they only fly in groups during migration. They are found primarily in once-volcanic tropical and mountainous habitats. Except during migration periods, they tend to hole up, like the larger flightless dragons, in volcanic craters, caves, and deep mountainous canyons.

LAKE DRAGONS

This group includes some large and little-known creatures that spend virtually their entire lives in the water, usually in freshwater lakes with outlets to the sea, where they sometimes migrate when the lakes freeze over or become otherwise uninhabitable. These great creatures are nothing but plesiosaurs, descendants of reptiles that inhabited the earth during the age of dinosaurs. They are fish-eating reptiles, usually with a long neck, a small head with many sharp teeth, and paddle-legs that they use as oars and that enable them to swim forward and backward and to make quick turns in the water as they chase their prey. There are both long-necked and short-necked fossil types, but only the long-necked variety—sometimes reaching a length of fifty feet—survives today. The shorter-necked sort, or pliosaur, lived mostly on squids and molluscs and eventually died out. One of the most famous of lake dragons is the Loch Ness "monster."

Judging from observations made in North America, lake dragons are usually knobbed or horned on the top of the head, in a similar manner to the antlerlike structures found in the Oriental dragons. In Canada they have been seen most frequently at Lake Okanagan in British Columbia, where they are called Ogopogo, but they have been observed at other lakes in British Columbia, Manitoba, Ontario, and Quebec. They have also been spotted in Alaska and a dozen other states. Most of these lakes are very cold and deep, and some have connections to the sea by rivers or underground waterways. In Canada, the best places to observe these animals are in British Columbia (Lakes Okanagan, Cowichen, Pohengamok, and Shuswap). In the United States, Lake Payette in Idaho is the most famous site. However, Loch Ness in Scotland has the largest population of these dragons and is the best location to study them. Recent reports suggest that a separate population may also live in the upper reaches of the Congo basin, where the animals are known as the *mokele-mbembe* and are currently under investigation by a team of American zoologists.

LIFE HISTORIES

> *The dragons begin to speak; yin and yang are commingled.*
>
> Yuen Kien Lei Han

FLIGHT AND MIGRATION

The best information we have on the flight behavior of dragons comes from radar data of the U.S. military, which keeps close tabs on all air movement between the Asian and North American continents. The first radar detections of migrating dragons caused considerable consternation and set off a SAC warning of an imminent attack by Soviet bombers, which nearly provoked a retaliatory launch of 1325 ICBMs. However, when a squadron of jets took off at midnight to intercept the invading planes, nothing could be seen. Radar blips indicated a group of objects moving at thirty miles per hour in close formation and flying at a height of 4500 feet, but they were much too small to be either missiles or bombers. It was too dark to make out the appearance of the creatures in any detail, but a fighter pilot who caught a glimpse of one said that it looked like a "giant bat." After that embarrassing encounter, which cost the government an estimated $25,000,000 in wasted military maneuvers, the radar sets were recalibrated to screen out all objects flying at less than fifty miles an hour, on the assumption that no nation would try attacking the United States using missiles or aircraft flying at such low speeds. However, a supersecret study was at once undertaken by the Air Force to look into the feasibility of capturing dragons and training them to drop miniature germ-warfare bombs on the Asian continent, in order to spread panic and disease among the populace.

As a result of the Freedom of Information Act, radar data on the flight behavior of dragons have been obtained from the Air Force files. The highlights can be summarized here without seriously endangering the nation's security, although military authorities have warned us about the possible misuse of this information, should it fall into the wrong hands.

We now know that dragons can stay aloft for at least twenty-four hours at a time, that they normally take flight shortly after sunset, and that their flights peak at about midnight. They usually land before sunrise; they typically cover about four hundred to five hundred miles per night. They like to fly

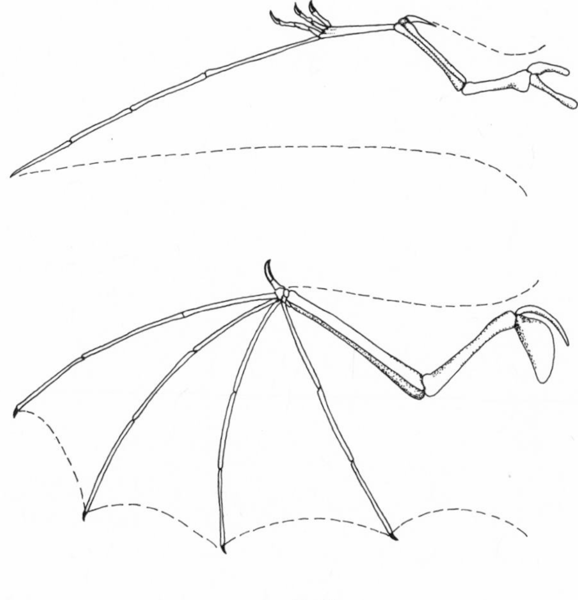

with tailwinds and prefer to fly when skies are cloudless. They evidently use celestial navigation, guided especially by such stars as Thuban and the North Star. Except during spring and fall migrations, which occur in late May and in September, dragons do not fly in groups; but during those migrations they will sometimes fly in phalanx formation, usually in the form of a broad V. Adult dragons always fly at the head of the formation, and youngsters take up the rear. In the fall, when there are usually several youngsters in a group, the flock rarely flies above one thousand feet and stops often.

Dragons take off from a running start and require a rather long and flat "runway," since their wings are relatively long and fragile—bushes or other vegetation can seriously impede takeoffs. At times, dragons also launch themselves from cliffs and treetops. They seem to enjoy flying in the updrafts of onshore winds against seashore cliffs. In such updrafts they can rise several thousand feet in only a few minutes and may remain aloft for hours on end, soaring in great circles far out of sight of humans.

FOODS AND GENERAL BEHAVIOR

It is quite fair to say that in spite of all that has been written about dragons, none have in reality proven to be intentional man-eaters, and indeed few of these remarkable creatures are flesh-eaters at all. To be sure, the lake dragons live mostly on fish, and when they are at sea they will sometimes eat squid and octopus but they have never been known to attack shipwrecked sailors or other persons lost at sea.

The smaller flying dragons are omnivorous and consume fruits and berries of various kinds, including gooseberries, raspberries, and wild plums. They sometimes fly up into tall nut-bearing trees, such as beech and walnut trees, to gather the nut crop. On occasion, they will steal the eggs from birds' nests, and they also enjoy eating mushrooms, which often grow in their weyrs.

The diets of the large flightless dragons are of special concern to us, and various studies based on the analysis of dragon scat and direct observation now provide us with conclusive evidence of their foraging behavior. They feed mostly at night, since, like all dragons, they avoid bright light. They are tall enough to feed on the leaves of trees that are above the reach of deer or other large mammals. They like the buds, leaves, and seeds of many kinds of hardwood trees but are especially fond of aspens and cottonwoods. All of these are rich in sugars and other nutritious materials and have few of the oils and bitter tastes of coniferous vegetation. Thus, flightless dragons are much more common in areas of hardwood vegetation than in coniferous forests, and their foraging activities are often evident there. In fact, like beavers, they often gnaw off small aspens near their bases, leaving only the larger parts of the trunk. They carry the larger branches to their weyrs to be eaten, when required, in peace and quiet during the daylight hours. However, their teeth are, of course, much smaller than those of beavers, and an experienced naturalist can easily tell beaver cuttings from those of dragons.

The large amount of woody materials in the diets of the flightless dragons have resulted in a specialized metabolism. All dragons of this type have modified their stomachs to allow bacterial fermentation to break down lignin, cellulose, and other woody materials. The chemistry of this metabolism is very similar to that of termites, and sometimes dragons are forced to eat termites to replenish the supply of cellulose-digesting bacteria in their stomachs. Because of the long fermentation period, it is believed that dragons eat only once a week, consuming several hundred pounds of leafy materials at one feeding, then returning to their lairs to sleep and rest for several days as their digestion proceeds. The amount of gases produced during this process is enormous. Luckily for the dragon, its otherwise keen sense of smell is immune to these fumes, which include hydrogen sulfide as well as methane.

Dragons are by far the most intelligent of all reptiles and have a remarkably large brain. They have an excellent memory and can remember for decades—if not centuries—the locations of especially good stands of favorite foods. Dragons spend much of their spare time scratching on the walls of their caves, and some of these scratches are clearly pictured representations of their lives

and environments. In fact, some of the cave "art" that humans have attributed to early man are almost certainly the work of dragons. These drawings are primarily animals that dragons fear, such as elephants and lions, both of which have been at war with dragons for centuries. However, the drawings also include representations of their own kind, often depicted in a stylized and heroic fashion. This has led some authorities to believe that dragons may possess a religious sense and a concept of a Supreme Dragon which they worship. Interestingly, even flightless dragons often depict their own kind with large wings, soaring upward from the earth; this may suggest a concept of heaven or paradise.

In general, adult dragons are not very playful, although youngsters, or dragonlings, like to play king-of-the-hill and similar games that improve physical coordination and skills. A young dragon will sometimes "play dead" and let some other creature walk up and begin investigating. Then, without warning, the dragon will stand up, spread its wings, and hiss loudly, frightening the poor creature witless. Young dragons also mimic other creatures, assuming the posture of a perched eagle or vulture, or camouflaging themselves, changing color to resemble a large stump and blend into the background. These are usually protective devices, used when humans approach and the animal is unable to escape.

SPECIAL SENSES

The hearing of dragons is remarkable. Besides the normal sonic range of humans, dragons have the ability to detect low-frequency infrasonic sounds and very high-frequency supersonic noises. Humans think of dragons as nearly voiceless. It seems to be true that dragons have limited sound-producing abilities within a human range of hearing. Besides hissing, they can clatter their teeth to frighten enemies; and in the case of the European species, even youngsters can release stomach gas with an explosive roar, whether or not it is ignited. Most humans assume that this is the full extent of dragon sounds. Yet, dragons can actually communicate not only at very high frequency ranges by vibration of special membranes in the throat, but also by extremely low frequency sounds resulting from contraction of special skin muscles that causes the body scales to vibrate and scrape over one another. This is an especially effective method for communication in swimming dragons. These low-frequency sounds carry for hundreds of miles in the water, and it is likely that all the dragons in the Caribbean are able to communicate with one another simultaneously by this unique mechanism. The high-frequency sound production technique is a short distance method of communicating used both on land and in flight.

Dragon eyesight is limited in that it is adapted to nighttime vision; all dragons are nearly color-blind. They are also dazzled by all bright lights and are thus unable to respond effectively when exposed to intense sunlight. When daylight approaches, dragons usually beat a hasty retreat to their weyrs. Each of the species of the large flightless dragon has a "third eye," or dracontia, in the middle of the forehead. This round, translucent body, believed in ancient times to be a valuable jewel, is actually a light detector that warns the dragon when overall light levels are becoming dangerously high for its real eyes.

Dragons also have a fine sense of smell. Their tongues are forked like those of snakes and are periodically extended into the air to "taste" for evidence of other dragons or of the proximity of humans. They are known to be able to detect the presence of humans in this way from a distance of at least one and eight-tenths miles and are therefore usually able to hide before humans come within eyesight.

BREATHING OF FIRE AND MIST

Perhaps the most remarkable behavior of the larger dragons is their ability to produce methane. We now know that all three of the large flightless dragons produce vast quantities of it and can emit a mixture of the gas and water vapor that resembles clouds or mist. But only the European dragon has evolved the means of igniting this vapor into an effective fire-breathing defensive tactic. Fire-breathing seems to be an innate behavior in European flightless dragons, dependent on their ability to strike sparks while belching forth stored methane from their special stomach compartment. Since few people have been close enough to dragons to see how this is accomplished—much less to live to tell the tale—we cannot be certain of the procedure. We surmise, however, that there is a powerful shutting of the jaws, which causes the teeth to strike each other so hard that a spark is produced, immediately igniting the released vapors. A flame-thrower effect is produced, capable of igniting everything within about twenty feet of the animal.

It is likely that fire-breathing is an ancient ability of dragons, for some of the fossil remains of *Mesodraco* show charring around the front teeth, suggesting that it too was able to produce fire. Yet, the teeth remains of *Protodraco* seem untouched by fire, so it is likely that fire-breathing originated more recently than *Protodraco*'s time, or about one hundred million years ago. From this, one concludes that dragons knew how to produce and use fire long before man, who has been familiar with fire for only about a million years. In fact, it is quite possible that man learned how to use fire for cooking food by seeing fire-breathing dragons (at a safe distance), finding and eating the charred remains of the animals the fire-breath had killed, and making the connection.

In this way, early man learned to depend on and exploit dragons; for a time humans even worshipped the creatures. Serpent worship and dragon cults were popular in Egypt about the time the Jewish religion was being formalized. The many references in the Old Testament to the evil characteristics of serpents and dragons were thus simply a way to contain and counteract this undesirable influence. The use of the image of a serpent with great knowledge and mystical healing qualities has nonetheless been unwittingly passed down to the present day by the medical profession in the form of the caduceus. Early Christians, always looking for morality symbols, found in the dragon the perfect symbol of evil, death, and destruction. So the reputation of dragons as intelligent creatures worthy of reverence eventually changed to inspire fear and loathing. Gradually dragon slaying came to be the most honored of all manly endeavors; dragons retreated before man's onslaught and spent an increasing amount of their time hidden in dark caves and secret places.

ENEMIES

Clearly, man is the primary enemy of dragons and the major cause of their current scarcity. Humans have waged an ongoing battle with dragons for at least two thousand years, and as a result dragons have become both rare and elusive. The other major enemy of the dragon is the elephant, as has been mentioned. The natural enmity between dragons and elephants has been known for centuries; even Pliny referred to the terrible battles these beasts waged. More recently, fighting has moved increasingly into the philosophical arena, with the elephants defending traditional values and attitudes against attacks by the more unpredictable dragons.

Elephants and dragons eat many of the same foods, and both require prodigious amounts to survive. Fights over limited food sources were probably always commonplace and eventually led to an abiding hatred between the two kinds of animals. Dragons are quite content to leave elephant herds alone during the day, for they could easily be trampled to death or impaled on the elephant's long tusks. At night, however, the odds are different. By holding its breath until the right moment, so as not to give itself away by the smell of stomach gases, a dragon can sneak up close to a lone elephant, surprise the animal with fire-breath, and burn the elephant to death before retaliation is possible. Dragons rarely eat the elephants they kill but are said to drink the blood to gain strength. No wonder dragons often dream of elephants and scratch crude pictographs of them on the walls of their caves!

Dragons do not get along well with lions or panthers, either, and have let it be known that they feel they have been mistreated by the news media.

REPRODUCTION AND LONGEVITY

It is probably true that most estimates of dragon longevity are exaggerations; many believed that dragons live for thousands of years. Nevertheless, dragons are very long-lived. Once a dragon reaches its adult size, it is not terribly vulnerable to attack by any creature except man. Dragons grow more rapidly in summer than in winter, when they are less active (they have been known to hibernate in some areas); the growth rate of their scales changes with the seasons. As a result, one can examine a dragon's scale under a microscope and estimate the dragon's age, in the same way that trees can be dated by their rings or fishes by their scales. Only a few dragon scales have thus been studied, but the number of annual growth rings has usually been found to number between four hundred and five hundred, suggesting that at least several centuries would represent an average lifespan for an adult dragon. Many dragons simply die of old age; they become too infirm to get around easily, and their teeth wear down to the gums, so that they can no longer chew up woody food.

It requires a century or so for dragons to reach sexual adulthood, when the rudimentary wings of the males become more brightly patterned, and the females turn an alluring tone of golden yellow on their undersides. At that time the females also begin to exude a musky odor from special glands under their chins, and males are able to detect these odors through hundreds of miles of water or dozens of miles of air. The mating season is in the late spring, and it is then that dragons are most likely to be seen or heard by humans, as they become so preoccupied with mating that they lose much of their habitual wariness.

The mating displays of dragons no doubt vary

among the several different species and have been observed by only a few trained biologists. Among the flying dragons, both sexes perform synchronized aerial displays while facing one another, and the male performs looping or falling-leaf shows and spectacular dives from great heights, finally pulling out and zooming over the female's head while she watches from the ground. Displays in the flightless species are obviously much less spectacular but also involve the exposure of the brilliantly patterned wings, which are waved about as the male jumps and leaps. This mating display often lasts for hours, as the male dances his way around the female. Great circular impressions are made in the ground from his continuous wild movements. The origin of these circular markings, or roundeleys, has often been mistakenly attributed to prehistoric human activities. The female dragon meanwhile thumps her tail on the ground, in time with the dancelike movements of the male.

Traditional display grounds are usually barren hillsides or even mountaintops, where the visibility is unrestricted and where the light of the morning sun strikes first. The display begins well before dawn and continues until the sunlight is so intense that the animals must retire to darker places. Most actual mating probably occurs before sunrise or during twilight hours.

Traditional display grounds are used by dragons for centuries. In England, these circular display grounds are often found in particular geographic alignments, or dragon-leys, which connect various hilltops (dragon weyrs) and stone circles. These stone circles have been erected by early dragon-worshipping cults, to help commemorate traditional display sites, and perhaps to attract new dragons to the area. A few similar stone circles have also been found in Montana and other parts of the mountainous American West, suggesting that similar dragon cults probably existed in these places as well.

Displays go on at the dragon arenas for several weeks, until the dragoness has been fertilized. Then she retires to her weyr to await the laying of her eggs. In the large flightless dragons of Europe and America, the female lays a small clutch of three or four eggs, which are about the size of grapefruits, pure white, and shiny as pearls. As the young dragon embryo grows within, the egg gradually turns to a beautiful golden hue, looking for all the world like true gold. No doubt this is the basis for the nearly universal belief that dragons hoard and stand guard over great treasures of gold and pearls. Certainly a clutch of eggs would appear to be a vast treasure to the average observer, and the anger of a nesting female dragon at being disturbed is easily imagined. The incubation period of the eggs is about three months. When the young are about to hatch, the female wraps her body even more closely around the eggs to keep them warm and safe. Probably the reason that dragons prefer to lay their eggs in the craters of dormant volcanoes is that the craters are often still slightly warm and so provide a perfect incubator for the eggs. Otherwise, the dragoness must warm them with her own body and that of decaying leafy materials she piles up around the eggs when she leaves the clutch to feed.

The hatchlings quickly peck their way out of their shells and can crawl about immediately. They are simply miniature versions of the adults, and even at hatching the males can be easily recognized by their tiny winglike forelegs. They are fed insects and berries by their mother, who goes out each night to gather the food. Within a few weeks the hatchlings begin to follow her outside, usually riding on her back, and sometimes sliding down her tail in a playful way. By the time they are a few months old they are several feet long and begin to move around independently. It should be noted that the male plays very little part in the care and raising of the brood and after mating often moves on to look for other mates. His absence probably helps to keep the location of the breeding weyr unknown, and so contributes indirectly to the breeding success. In any case, the female is quite able to protect the dragonlings herself.

Youngsters of the larger species leave the mother's weyr near the end of the first year of life, or just before the start of the next breeding season, and venture out on their own. They are then about six feet long, and relatively safe from most predators, except perhaps lions and panthers. They avoid these animals and, of course, stay away from elephants at all costs. Females are always flightless but can reach the lower branches of tall trees, and the males, even of the flightless species, are able at this point in their lives to fly up into the higher branches. So the fledgling dragons go off on their own and remain quite solitary until they become sexually mature about ninety-nine years later. As the males grow larger they too become flightless and usually quite sedentary.

SOCIAL ORGANIZATION AND JUSTICE

Dragons live in a complex society that reflects their great intelligence and strong sense of justice. Their

A Prayer for Our Veterans

Oh God, Our Heavenly Father,
You have blessed us with
brave men and women
who are willing to defend our freedom.
May Your protection and grace
surround them each day.
Let Your healing hand be upon those
who suffer wounds and injuries.
May those who have made the
ultimate sacrifice rest forever in
Your Holy Presence.
Comfort the families who mourn
and are left to remember
the precious lives of their loved ones.
Help us to honor and support them.
Let us ever be mindful of each sacrifice made
on behalf of the American people by our
sons, daughters, husbands, wives, mothers,
fathers, and friends.
Amen

social order is determined entirely by age and size, the oldest and wisest among them being of the highest social rank. Such old and venerated dragons are called pendragons, and their opinions carry great authority. Dragons of either sex can be pendragons; there is no sexual discrimination in this matter.

Periodically, all the adults of each dragon dominion gather at traditional meeting places, usually large craters, to meet and discuss current issues and to revise the Draconic Code. These periodic assemblages, or dragon senates, are times when matters of great concern are dealt with. In recent years, as the dragon population has become extremely low, it has rarely been possible for the dragons to meet formally in such senates. As a result, many of the younger dragons are losing interest in traditional methods of discussing and settling matters of general draconian interest. There has thus been a decreasing respect for the basic principles of dragon culture and an increasing amount of wanton destruction of property and unprovoked attacks on humans. Naturally, such renegade dragons have been punished appropriately, when possible, by being placed in solitary confinement for two centuries or more on small, remote tropical islands, with no visiting privileges. This is bitter punishment indeed, for dragons are highly intellectual creatures and tend to pine away when separated from all aspects of dragon culture.

One current and extremely serious problem facing dragon society is the recent effort on the part of some dragon dominions to attain economic and military superiority over other dominions. The issue mainly concerns the presumed threat posed by the European dragon, which possesses the ultimate offensive weapon, fire-breathing. Both the American and Oriental dragon populations have begun to invest in the appropriate technology to attain this dreadful weaponry, and both populations are now sufficiently scientifically advanced to be able to convert their normal respiratory processes and achieve igniting capabilities. So far, calmer heads have prevailed, and the FACT (Fire-Breathing Avoidance Consensus Treaty) stands. Yet some more volatile individuals from the American dragon population consider themselves at a serious strategic disadvantage with the current treaty and believe it important to negotiate from a position of technological and military equality, if not superiority. The Oriental dragons take a similar stand. Unless there is a prolonged period of negotiations, there is real danger of international warfare breaking out over misinterpreted motives, which would mean the end of all dragon culture as it is known today. Even some of the smaller dragon species, which at present do not breathe pure methane, are considering changing their food priorities. They intend to cut back on their current nutritional budget and to convert to a high-cellulose diet in order to attain fire-breathing capabilities. The desire for such fire-breathing capability is rampant, and we can only hope that dragons are sufficiently intelligent to recognize before it is too late the futility of warfare as a means of proving military strength.

What are the four Intelligent Creatures?
The unicorn, the phoenix, the tortoise, and the dragon.
Traditional Chinese Saying

II. DRAGONS AND MAN

And this which I have written, may be sufficient to satisfy any reasonable man that there are winged serpents and dragons in the world.

Edward Topsell, 1658

The Dragons of Antiquity

As mentioned earlier, humans and dragons have lived in proximity to one another for a million years or more. It was probably on the African plains that the earliest humans first learned about the use of fire for cooking food by watching dragons. However, we have very little knowledge or information about these early encounters. We do know, as mentioned, that by the time of the early Egyptian period a considerable dragon- and serpent-worshipping cult had developed. This cult gradually spread to Babylon, India, the Orient, the Pacific Islands, and finally the North American continent, as more and more cultures began to recognize and appreciate the special powers and intelligence of dragons. The cult reached its peak during the days of the Roman Empire and disappeared with the advent of Christianity. Gradually the concept of a mother goddess, often in serpent form, was replaced with a father figure who was distinctly antidragon.

Well before the time of Christ, when dragons were still common in northern Europe, they began to compete with primitive men for caves to live in. One type of caveman, who inhabited the Neanderthal Valley, had a particular mystical association with dragons. Although all the evidence indicates that they belonged to a less intelligent race of early man than other types living in the vicinity, these cave dwellers regarded themselves as genetically superior by virtue of the special powers bestowed on them by dragons. They referred to their leader as the Great Dragon, and every spring they gathered on hillsides and made great bonfires to imitate dragon fires. During these ceremonies they drank "dragon blood," a primitive wine made from the juices of grapes, and burned their enemies in effigy. They considered aggression and strength to be much greater virtues than intelligence and only allowed the strongest among them to reproduce. Eventually their preoccupation with physical strength became so overwhelming that only males were allowed to marry. The race died out a few decades later. Our only real evidence of their culture comes from a few skeletons, some crude scratches on cave walls, and the accounts of the more advanced races of humans who observed their behavior and considered them some primitive type of troll.

Farther north, dragons were especially common in the mountains of Scandinavia. One of the most feared of the early Nordic dragons was named Nidhoggr, or the "dread biter." He lived for thousands of years and was believed to have spent most of that time gnawing at the root of the universal tree of life, a gigantic ash tree that supported all the living realms. But most of the dragons of Scandinavian lore were large aquatic creatures that lived off the coasts among the swirling waters. It was said that these aquatic dragons, or Krakens, lifted their enormous heads and long necks out of the water to seize sailors right off their ships. Much of the supposed violence caused by the Scandinavian dragons, however, has been confused with that wreaked by the plundering Vikings, who usually placed a dragon's head on the figureheads of their great ships. Their victims believed that an actual dragon had come to destroy them. Thus, as on numerous occasions, dragons were blamed for the evils that mankind had brought upon itself.

Perhaps the largest and most famous dragon of all time was Typhon, who lived in ancient Greece. It was so large that its head was said to reach the stars, and its wings were so broad that they could block the sunlight. Its roaring was like that of a terrible storm, and from its mouth came not only flame but coughed-up rocks. When it belched forth its fire, even the gods of Olympus were forced to flee. Finally Zeus turned on the monster and slew it. The carcass was eventually buried under Mount Etna, which even today occasionally sends forth smoke, suggesting that the creature did not die after all but is only awaiting the right time to rise again. The windstorms that Typhon produced when enraged are commemorated in the word "typhoon," which, like the *Huracan* of the Caribbean islands, reminds us of the terrible powers of the great pendragons.

In spite of this unfavorable example, serpent-dragons were believed by the Greeks to be great sources of knowledge and wisdom and were considered sacred creatures with oracular abilities by both Greeks and Romans. Small nonvenomous snakes were commonly kept in Roman households, where they no doubt kept the mouse and rat population in check and were called *dracunculi,* or "little dragons." Treated as pets, they slept in various nooks and crannies and were fed at the table like dogs or cats. Serpents were to be found at shrines, where they transmitted their great wisdom through the mouths of priestesses. Python was the name of one such serpent-dragon, who guarded the shrine at Delphi until he was killed by Apollo. Another dragon, named Ladon, faithfully guarded a tree of golden apples (perhaps a clutch of golden eggs?) that belonged to Hera; and the apples contained the secrets of knowledge and immortality. One of the many tasks of Hercules was to kill this dragon and bring back a few of the apples to King Eurystheus. It is from this encounter that we can trace the popular image of dragons as the guardians of great treasures and the custodians of forbidden knowledge. The great battle between Ladon (or Draco) and Hercules is forever enshrined in the constellations of the northern skies, where Hercules may be seen trying to step on the dragon's head.

Unfortunately the story is told a little differently in the Old Testament. In this version, the "dragon"—the serpent—did not guard the tree of life and knowledge but slyly tempted Eve to eat the apples, resulting, of course, in the expulsion of both Adam and Eve from the Garden of Eden. Thanks to Genesis, the dragon/serpent became the symbol of temptation, and humans, recalling other legends of the dragon's destructiveness, were provided with ample excuse to seek out and kill every dragon in the land. Dragons soon disappeared from Greek and Roman homes and oracles, and were no longer available for transmitting their wisdom to those who wanted to learn from them. The total decay of the Greek and Roman civilizations followed inexorably. For many centuries thereafter, as the Dark Ages descended on Europe, dragons were greatly feared. Fortune seekers, vainly hunting for the treasures of gold that they thought the dragons guarded, sought out breeding weyrs and stole dragon eggs, and many a knight tried to impress his girlfriend by slaying a dragon or two.

Dragon Slayers of Medieval Times

One of the earliest known dragon slayers was the warrior Siegfried (in the Teutonic version), or Sigurd (Scandinavian version), who lived so long ago that the facts of his dragon-battle are greatly muddled. Some people believe that he slew the dragon Fafnir to rescue a captive maiden; in other accounts he was simply looking for treasure. Some centuries earlier, in England,

Beowulf took on a similar dragon but was fatally wounded in the resulting battle. Clearly, the weapons and methods used by these early warriors were not always equal to the task.

The first really epic battle between man and dragon that comes down to us in any detail is that of Saint George. He lived before the time of Constantine and was probably born in Palestine. During one of his travels, he came to the city of Silene (or Sisena) in Libya. There he learned of a dragon, living in a nearby lake, that was reputedly raiding neighboring pastures and eating the sheep. After all the sheep had disappeared, the townspeople found it necessary to offer up all their children to the dragon, until only the daughter of the king remained. By the time George arrived on the scene, even the king's daughter had been bound up and was about to be offered to the creature. Without delay the good knight attacked the surprised dragon with his lance. He quickly bound the dragon up with the princess's girdle (although never adequately explaining to the king how that item of clothing had come off). He led the cowering beast back to the city, where he killed it by slicing off its head in a single blow, in view of the entire populace. In spite of this good deed, George eventually came to an unhappy end. According to some accounts, he tore down and impulsively stamped on an edict that had been issued by the Roman emperor Diocletian. For this foolhardy act he was arrested and eventually put to death. Others said that he was decapitated by the emperor of Persia for trying to convert the emperor's wife to Christianity. Clearly he didn't have the good sense to stay away from the wives and daughters of royalty, and he was probably not greatly missed until he was made a saint some centuries later. In 1349 he was even made the patron saint of England. He was also given honorary if posthumous citizenship there, since it had by then been decided that he had actually been born in Coventry. In the sixteenth century, Pope Clement VII decreed that George had not been completely truthful about his dragon-killing stories, and the pope decided to eliminate all mention of dragons from St. George's official biography. More recently, poor George was even decanonized, and the arguments over which cathedral actually possesses his head and other bodily parts have gradually diminished.

Not nearly so well known as George was another dragon killer of the Dark Ages by the name of Gerolde. He acquired during his lifetime a large and faithful following of people eager to hear of his dragon-slaying exploits. For many years he roamed the countryside seeking dragons and other evil creatures, speaking out against them, and burning any books that mentioned dragons or their kin. He was eventually made a knight and was dubbed Gerolde-the-Good, because of his obvious piety. His minions formed what was probably the first fan club in history and referred to themselves as the pious multitude, whose major goal was to seek out and destroy sin in all of its many forms.

The first dragon that Gerolde slew was a relatively small one (evidently only about twenty feet long) that he managed to surprise one day while dressed in his shiniest suit of armor and riding his charger. Without a thought for his own safety, he attacked the beast. The reflections of the sun off shiny armor dazzled the dragon, and before it could retaliate, it found itself fatally impaled on Gerolde's long lance. Gerolde was immediately hailed as the greatest of all dragon killers, and he was swamped with requests to speak before civic groups and to clear dragons out of various strongholds. He traveled about the land with his entourage and was offered rich presents and rewards for his good deeds. Among these were numerous brightly colored silk garlands and ribbons, which well-wishers begged he would attach to his lance or his helmet for good fortune. Finally, Gerolde had the clever idea of making an entire multicolored jacket of these ribbons, which he could slip over his armored suit. He was immediately transformed into a flaglike vision of blue, white, red, and green. Shortly thereafter, clad in his colorful garment, he encountered a large dragon and attacked it with full confidence in his invulnerability. This time the reflective armor was effectively hidden by the jacket, and the sun was hidden by clouds. The dragon, upon being attacked, released a vast amount of fire, incinerating Gerolde on the spot. His followers were badly shaken by this turn of events but nevertheless recovered his charred remains and returned to town. He was buried in a nearby cathedral, with all possible honors. On his grave a simple epitaph was engraved in Latin*, which in translation reads: "Never wrap yourself in a flag when you go forth to slay dragons."

Dragons of the Late Middle Ages and Renaissance

By the end of the Middle Ages and the beginning of the Renaissance, a goodly number of dragon slayers had hacked their way into history, and many had been made saints in the process. The killing of dragons had become one of the few suitable

***Numquam gerite signum ubi draconem petitis.*

occupations for women, who had discovered that dragons were not only susceptible to lance and spear but could be rendered helpless by the mere sight of a crucifix or, in fact, of any shiny, reflective object. Thus, Saint Margaret of Antioch, when she was thrown into prison and approached by a dragon she believed had dishonorable intentions, simply whipped out her silver cross and held it in front of the beast. Almost immediately the dragon was transformed into a cowering hulk and thereafter followed her meekly about like a tame dog.

In his natural history of four-footed beasts, serpents, and insects, published in the 1600s, Edward Topsell considered the dragon a kind of serpent and located it alphabetically between the double-headed serpent, or *Amphisbaena,* and the *Dryine,* a highly venomous serpent. Most of Topsell's information on serpents and dragons actually came from an earlier summary by Conrad Gesner, and neither man had much to add about dragons that had not been previously known. Yet Topsell recounted several stories of affection between men and dragons, proving that earlier attitudes about the basic enmity between humans and dragons were weakening. Thus he noted that "savage dragons are made loving and tame to men, by good turns and benefits bestowed upon them, for there is no nature which may not be overcome by kindness."* He also reported a case of a boy and a dragon who were raised as playmates. The boy grew up, and the two separated; the dragon returned to the woods. Later, traveling through the wood where the dragon lived, the man was fallen upon by thieves. The dragon, hearing the man's calls for help, rushed to his friend and dispatched the thieves. The dragon accompanied his friend out of the woods to safety. Dragons had also

*Topsell, vol. 2, p. 709.

been found to honor virginity; it was learned they could instinctively recognize a virgin when they saw one, which made them useful arbiters of justice. But dragons also suffered some bad publicity during the Renaissance. African explorers sent back very unfavorable accounts of horrid, monstrous dragons, which damaged the beasts' image considerably in Europe.

At about this time, a considerable number of dragons were found still living in the Swiss Alps, especially near Mount Pilatus. A barrelmaker from Lucerne stumbled on one dragon weyr when he fell into a deep cavern on a late fall day. The two dragons living inside were preparing for winter and entering a state of semihibernation. The barrelmaker decided to spend the winter there with the dragons and actually remained there from early November until nearly the middle of the following April. At that time the dragons again became active; as one left the cave the barrelmaker grabbed hold of its tail and thus escaped. His remarkable adventure was later immortalized by a monument in the Church of Saint Leodegaris in Lucerne.

But many Europeans were beginning to doubt that dragons had ever existed at all. By the 1700s, dragons were so rare in Europe that large rewards were being offered for complete specimens, and the great biologist Carl von Linne refused to include any dragons in his list of known animal species. This was a bitter blow to dragon lovers and only reinforced the growing skepticism about the existence of dragons, which has carried down to the present day.

Recent Dragon Sightings

In recent years there have been relatively few sightings of flying dragons—although as the rate of dragon sightings has declined, sightings of Unidentified Flying Objects have increased. There can be little doubt that at least some of these UFOs are actually flying dragons, as indicated by the following lines of evidence:

1. Nearly all UFOs are seen at night, when dragons are normally aloft.
2. Most UFO sightings occur in spring and fall—the seasons for dragon migration—in the Northern Hemisphere, their preferred habitat. Very few UFOs have been seen in the Southern Hemisphere, where no flying dragons are known to breed today. One of the few known areas of historic dragon activity in the Southern Hemisphere is on the Nazca plain of Peru, where there are

many signs of previous dragon display activity and sacred dragon gatherings. Large pictographic patterns in the earth are also clearly in the forms of large flightless dragons and flying "angelic" dragons. This site once may have represented a major gathering place for dragons, but they have since abandoned the area.

3. Many sightings of UFOs are associated with mountaintops or hills in open country, which are, of course, favored locations for dragon weyrs and display grounds.

4. Many UFOs glow in the dark, or produce bright lights in the sky. This is certainly related to the fact that flying dragons exhale large amounts of methane, which can be ignited by lightning or by other electrical effects of the atmosphere. Some of the better displays of northern lights, which generally appear in the northern sky in early fall, are probably attributable to the atmospheric effects of large dragon flights between Alaska and Siberia.

In the face of so much evidence, it is clear that many of the current theories explaining UFOs—visitations of angels or extraterrestrial beings and so on—will have to be reconsidered and the much more probable explanations of dragons taken into account. The U.S. military has the best information on dragons and UFOs but has, regrettably, been unwilling to release its best dragon data, most of which are still highly classified.

Myths and Misconceptions

TREASURE HOARDING

Like child eating, the myth of gold hoarding by dragons is an ancient one, based on a slight amount of evidence that has been greatly abused and misconstrued. We already know that dragons and serpents often were used to guard temples and other sacred places by the ancient Greeks and Romans and that as a result they were associated with the presence of something valuable. As far back as the seventh or eighth century A.D., the dragon was believed to be a hoarder of great treasure, as is indicated by the Old English epic of *Beowulf*. In many cultures, as mentioned earlier, European dragons were believed to carry a magical stone imbedded in their forehead, the dracontia. In the case of the Oriental dragon, a pearl-like or golden, globular object was often depicted being held directly below the chin, or suspended in the air in front of it. We have already suggested that the object is no doubt a dragon egg. Some have thought, however, that this object represented the moon or the sun and that the dragon's action of carrying it symbolized the creature's great powers. Others confused the beautiful eggs with gigantic pearls or rounded golden nuggets.

Only a few authentic dragon eggs have ever been collected and displayed at museums, but there are many fake dragon eggs that even today exist in major collections. These fakes are made of a highly glazed porcelain and are almost impossible to tell from the real thing without chemical analysis. They always have a small hole drilled in one end, through which the supposed contents have been removed; but the holes are generally too small to have allowed for the drainage of the real dragon contents, especially in the later "golden" stages. True dragon eggs, on the other hand, usually show some slight staining on their glossy surface, and the drain holes are somewhat larger. They are nearly as thick and hard as the porcelain fakes, and it is hard to imagine how the dragonling is able to chip its way out at the time of hatching. On the average, the shells are about 9.9 inches long, 9.6 inches wide, and 0.5 inches thick, and they are slightly oval—the fakes are typically round. In some of the authentic golden-stage eggs, details of the dead embryo can be seen by X-rays, and this area deserves much additional study. One such egg is in a museum in Turin, Italy. Although under constant guard, it has been particularly well scrutinized recently by advanced scientific techniques such as mass spectrometry and is now known to be the only authentic golden-stage dragon egg in any museum collection.

CHILD STEALING

Probably one of the most widely held misconceptions of dragons is the belief that they habitually capture children and maidens—particularly maidens—and carry them off to devour. Indeed, much of the fear and loathing of dragons stems from this attitude, which is very old indeed. As we know from the reputed exploits of Saint George, the people of Silene, Libya, used to tie up their children and place them out in the fields to be eaten by the dragon that lived in the swamp nearby. When they found the children dead and half-eaten a few days later, they believed the dragon had consumed them; they did not consider the possibility that other wild predatory animals might be dwelling in the vicinity. Many of these child-sacrifice rites no doubt can be traced back to the Book of Revelations, in which it is stated that "a great red dragon, having seven heads and ten horns, and seven crowns upon his head" stood before a woman ready to give birth, waiting to devour the child as soon as it was born. It is clear from this description that no actual dragon could conceivably be blamed for this heinous crime, since no self-respecting dragon has ever been found with more than one head, and dragons are too democratic ever to wear crowns. Nevertheless, it became a tradition of the Ammonite people in early Palestine for the firstborn child to be sacrificed by fire to Moloch, a supposed dragon deity. Obviously it is unfair to blame dragons for such reprehensible behavior on the part of humans.

All recent evidence indicates that although dragons have occasionally been known to capture young children and carry them off, there is nothing to indicate that the dragons have ever done them any harm. Instead, dragons consider children ideal pets and playmates for the young dragonlings and invariably treat the human children as well as their own offspring. Dragonesses often construct little lean-to huts for the children to sleep in, gather mushrooms and berries for them to eat, and encourage them to cuddle up with the young dragonlings on cold nights. Preteenage humans are considered the best playmates for baby dragons. They eat nearly the same foods and are about the same size, so that they can enter into most of the dragon games on an equal basis. Invariably, the children are released unharmed when the dragonlings approach independence, toward the end of summer, and are always set free near their human homes. Very few children, though, ever divulge to their parents where they have been or what they have been doing all summer. They know that their parents would be inclined to send the police and militia out to hunt down and kill the dragon families, despite their pleas. In fact, few children are willing to talk of their experiences at all, since their adventures are never believed by their friends, and they soon learn that it is better to keep quiet or simply say that they spent the summer at their grandparents' home than to tell the truth.

In a few cases "dragon-children" have kept diaries or have written down their memories in later years, and it is clear from such evidence that these people have usually considered their dragon-summer to have been the best summer they ever spent, since they didn't have to mow the lawn, wash dishes, or scrub the floors. Mother dragons are reportedly remarkably good housekeepers, and their weyrs are kept spotlessly clean. Some children are initially upset about eating from the floor of the cave rather than at tables and about the lack of silverware, but they soon come to think of the whole experience as a gigantic camping trip. (Most, however, do find it awkward to adjust to the dragon's daily schedule, since dragons tend to sleep during most of the daylight hours and perform all their foraging, play, and other activities at night.) Many of these dragon-children learned a great deal about self-reliance and independence during such summer sojourns, and all apparently came away with a greater love for nature. A few have become famous herpetologists as a result of their early experiences with dragons, and others have become active in the conservation movement, particularly in the recent attempts to establish dragon sanctuaries.

MEDICINAL USES OF DRAGON PARTS

Many parts of the dragon, such as the dracontia, the jewel-like third eye, were believed to provide effective antidotes for a wide array of poisons. The dracontia could be used repeatedly by boiling it in water; the water was drunk as a medicine. The fat of dragons, after being dried in the sun, was a known cure for ulcers. It also tended to repel a variety of undesirable beasts, including, perhaps, one's neighbors, and the heart was also greatly valued as a source of strength and intelligence.

Of all the parts of a dragon, none was more highly prized than its blood. The hero Sigurd, according to the thirteenth-century Scandinavian saga of the *Volsungs*, accidentally tasted the blood while roasting the heart of a dragon on a spit and was suddenly able to comprehend the language of birds. Drinking dragon's blood was believed to cure a variety of ailments, from blindness to kidney stones, and it was the only solution known by alchemists to be capable of dissolving gold, which made it valuable indeed. Dragon blood from the Yucatan population was found to be particularly powerful medicine and was fondly referred to by the few who could afford to buy it as "The Big Red." With the advent of the Industrial Revolution and the free-enterprise system, the commercial potential of dragons became obvious to many, and several dragon-hunting companies were formed. Expeditions were sent from Europe and the British Colonies to seek out all species of dragons, and it is at about this time that the populations of dragons began to decline precipitously. Many of these dragon hunters were wasteful in the extreme. Some cut out only the heart, leaving the rest to rot, while others drained the blood and ignored all the other useful portions. Still others gathered the teeth of the dragon, especially in the Orient, where it is widely believed that dragon teeth have great medicinal value.

Of course, unscrupulous merchants were not long in

discovering that dragon blood could easily be diluted with the blood of other creatures and still sold as the real thing. Two hundred–proof dragon blood became extremely rare, and many experiments were made to determine whether an easy test to judge the purity of dragon blood could be devised before it was purchased. It was discovered that eagle blood would not mix with dragon blood, and a market for eagle blood as a testing material soon developed. Just as rapidly, merchants began selling fake eagle blood. This, surprisingly enough, did not mix with fake dragon blood, and soon nearly everyone was profiting from the bonanza except the users of dragon blood.

Because of the efficacy of authentic dragon blood as a cure-all, it quickly became apparent that many physicians and drug manufacturers were likely to lose fortunes in consulting fees and pharmaceutical sales. Therefore, strong lobbying action was begun to place both real and fake dragon blood on the list of controlled substances. Word went out that dragon blood was highly addictive and could lead to early blindness and sterility if consumed too frequently. Soon it became illegal to deal in dragon blood on the open market, and so a thriving black market developed. At present, the official policy maintains that dragon blood is highly addictive and should only be given by special physicians in life-threatening situations. All other use of real or fake dragon blood is strictly prohibited by federal law, and a great deal of effort is being made to stamp out illegal use of the substances.

Protection and Conservation

Fortunately, ever since the passage of the Endangered Species Act of 1972, dragons have received federal protection in the United States, and the fines for killing dragons are now almost as severe as those associated with unlawful picketing of federal agencies. However, one serious loophole in the law exists. Because of lobbying pressures from egg collectors, dragon eggs are not yet provided with any protection. Egg collectors lure the dragoness from her weyr with jelly beans (of which dragons are inordinately fond) while a confederate enters the weyr and steals the eggs. Dragon eggs are the most beautiful and valuable of all eggs, and on the black market often fetch ten thousand dollars or more, especially for the later and more golden stages. This obviously places the activities of egg collectors on a collision course with conservationists.

Unfortunately, it is very difficult to tell a newly

fertilized dragon egg from an infertile one, and the latter certainly does not warrant protection in the view of either group. Yet, a few weeks after incubation, a simple test will distinguish fertilized from infertile eggs: the eggs can be submerged in water. Fertilized eggs will quickly rise to the surface, since the air chamber in the egg that surrounds the embryo reduces its specific gravity. Infertile eggs sink to the bottom and remain there. Few, if any, egg collectors are willing to make this test when they enter a dragon's weyr, for obvious reasons. Of course, the concerns and well-being of the mother dragon have never been taken into account by legislators trying to decide whether all dragon eggs should be protected.

The conservation of adult dragons is quite another question, and here nearly all biologists take the position that a series of refuges are needed in the ranges of all species if dragons are to survive. Areas that have been proposed as International Dragon Sanctuaries include: Loch Ness in Scotland and Lake Okanagan in British Columbia for the protection of the lake dragon; the vicinity of Mount Fiji and the streams and lakes at its base for the Oriental flightless dragon; the entire Yucatan Peninsula and the Caribbean from Cuba northward for the American flightless dragon. The European fire-breathing dragon is now so rare that nobody has been able to suggest a specific sanctuary, but the mountain ranges of northern Italy and the higher peaks of Greece are likely areas for consideration. The best sanctuary for the flying dragons of Asia would probably be the mountains of the Kamchatka Peninsula and the Koryak and Gydan ranges of the adjoining portions of Siberia. Political problems make it impossible to know to what extent protection is now being afforded dragons in this region. In North Korea, the flying dragon has been proposed as National Monument Number 425, and to disturb or kill one is punishable by death. This is harsh justice indeed, but the Koreans are to be commended for their special efforts to protect the flocks of flying dragons that still breed in their country.

Total dragon populations are impossible to judge at this point. It has been estimated, for example, that the American flightless dragon may now number no more than about twenty individuals. Some of these dragons are probably too old and others too young to breed, so it is possible that only a dozen breeding dragons of this type still exist. We must be thankful for their long lifespans; but since they lay only a few eggs each year, and many of these are stolen by egg collectors, the long-term outlook for the species is grim. Furthermore, dragons are still sometimes illegally captured and used for mock-warfare maneuvers by the military, who maintain that live dragons provide much better target practice for tanks than do nonliving targets and in addition give ground troops special reason for remaining alert at night. In spite of these sound reasons, we must condemn this unofficial policy of the military and hope that better substitute targets can be found in the future.

Wild dragons have never been successfully brought into captivity; it is not known whether they could or would ever adjust to such conditions. Some biologists have suggested taking a few eggs from the wild population and rearing the hatchlings under foster parents, such as vultures. Other scientists have suggested that the dragonlings be cared for by keepers in dragon costumes, so that the humans do not "imprint" unnatural parental stimuli on the young dragons. These dragon-parent surrogates would also have the responsibility for teaching the dragonlings the basics of draconian culture and providing them with religious training, including belief in a Supreme Dragon.

Apart from the collection of dragon eggs, the

only other major threat to the American dragon population at this time results from the lobbying efforts of a group calling themselves the National Dragon Slayers' Association. This group, formed before dragons came under the protection of the Endangered Species Act, consists primarily of persons who have actively hunted dragons in the past and would like to continue to do so without restriction. The association's membership requirements stipulate only that the applicant be an American citizen, preferably with an abiding hatred of dragons, devoted to the position that all Americans should have the right to bear arms suitable for the slaying of dragons, up to and including small tactical nuclear devices. The group would also like to abolish all existing dragon sanctuaries and prevent the possible registration of all dragon-killing weapons. Their official position is that America must be kept well armed and prepared for any possible dragon attack.

Although the position of the Dragon Slayer's Association seems somewhat extreme, the wealth and political power of this group cannot be underestimated. Already efforts are being made, thanks to the association's lobby, to exempt dragons from protection in particular areas through special legislation. Thus, dragons are no longer protected in many national forests. Their status in national parks has also been threatened because they compete with the beavers, deer, and other large, attractive animals tourists are most interested in seeing. Indeed, in a few national parks, dragons have been accused of carrying off and eating campers, when marauding bears were actually responsible. Thus there is considerable danger that some of the parks in the western mountain states, where the remnant American dragon populations are concentrated, may soon be opened to dragon hunting and the unlimited collection of dragon eggs. The Secretary of the Environment has recently taken the position that since the Bible specifically identifies dragons as evil creatures and associates them with the end of the world, it is senseless to protect dragons in national parks and thus perhaps inadvertently help to bring on the apocalypse.

On the other hand, dragons have received considerable support recently from the activities of a group calling itself Dragons Unlimited. It consists primarily of the well-to-do who hunted dragons for sport when it was still legal. These people now have devoted themselves to the restoration of dragon populations, in hopes that legal hunting seasons might be reestablished sometime in the future. Generous private donations, as well as membership fees, are being used to purchase and restore prime dragon-breeding habitats in Mexico, Canada, and the United States. In spite of the unfortunate long-range goal of the group, their efforts toward the conservation of dragon habitats must certainly be applauded.

The only good dragon is a dead dragon.
attributed to General George Custer

Current Controversies about Origins

In the past few years a heated argument has sprung up over the way in which the origins of dragons are presented in school textbooks. Biologists generally take the position, currently espoused by the prevailing texts, that all dragons evolved from reptilian ancestors, as outlined earlier in this book. They point to such strong evidence as the rather extensive fossil record, including such key transitional types as *Protodraco* and *Mesodraco,* and to the anatomical similarities between living dragons and all other extant types of reptiles.

On the other hand, some theologians believe that dragons were originally created in exactly the same form they have today and that they have not changed significantly in all the time they have been present on earth. Such persons point to the fact that dragons differ from all other living reptiles in several significant ways. First, no other reptile is known to have sexual differences in their number of ribs. Secondly, the extreme intelligence of dragons seems to be a God-given attribute, by comparison with the relative stupidity of all other reptiles. Third, dragons seem to be unique among animals (save man) in exhibiting true artistic abilities, a sense of the sublime, and a belief in immortality. These are indicated by the extensive amount of dragon art found in various dragon weyrs and near apparent dragon burial grounds. In fact, a special organization calling itself the Dragon Creation Study Center has recently been formed to further this viewpoint, and several states are considering legislation requiring the alteration of their textbooks to conform to it.

Some theologians have raised the issue of whether

or not the God who presumably listens to the pleas of mortal man can also hear the almost inaudible whispers of dragons or can understand the seemingly inchoate language of unicorns. At least some of these theologians have answered their own question with a definite "no." Many of these people do not even believe that dragons and unicorns possess souls, to say nothing of whether the creature's prayers are heard. Another question is whether there is one heaven for both dragons and unicorns, or a separate heaven for each, or if any heaven exists for either at all. If indeed there is a heaven anywhere, one can only hope that its gates are wide enough to accommodate the largest of all dragons and its horizons sufficiently remote to allow the shyest unicorn to graze in peace forever. Any "heaven" that has room only for those who subscribe to a rigid and limited set of beliefs is a fit place for those souls who deserve a very special kind of hell.

For the most part, we have made the beasts of fancy in our imagination more cruel and bloodthirsty . . . than the actual "lower animals." The dragons of the Western world do evil for evil's sake; the harpy is more terrible than the vulture, and the were-wolf is far more frightful than the wolf. Almost the only beast that kills for the pure joy of killing is Western civilized man, and he has attributed his own peculiar trait to the creatures of his imagination.

Odell Shepard, *The Lore of the Unicorn*

III. UNICORNS

God himself must needs be traduced, if there is no unicorn in the world.

Edward Topsell

The Evolution of Unicorns

Unicorns came upon the earth's scene much later than dinosaurs and dragons; it was not until well into the Age of Mammals, the Cenozoic Era, that the earliest unicorns appeared. They evolved not from horselike ancestors, as is generally believed, but from the order of cloven-hoofed mammals that includes present-day pigs, camel, deer, cows, sheep, goats, and antelope. This ancestry is evident for two reasons. First, unicorns have cloven hooves. Second, unicorns have true horns, which are only found among cloven-hoofed animals.

From this second point we can also conclude that unicorns belong to the antelope family rather than to the deer group. Deer antlers are bonelike

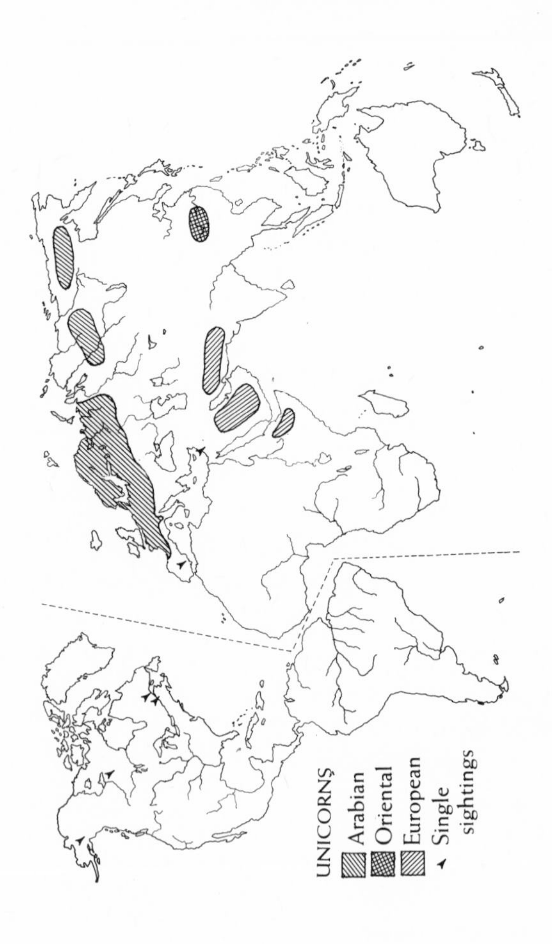
UNICORNS
Arabian
Oriental
European
Single sightings

structures that grow out of the forehead in the spring and summer of each year and are shed every winter. Antlers are usually grown only by males, although in a very few species the females also develop small antlers. Horns, such as are found in antelope, cattle, and sheep, are never shed but continue to grow throughout the animal's lifetime. Both sexes typically develop horns, with those of the males considerably larger. As this is the situation found in unicorns, we can be quite certain that the unicorns and true antelope evolved from a common ancestor. Unicorns may have first appeared in either Asia or northern Africa, both of which are current homes for true antelope.

The earliest cloven-hoofed mammal fossils date from Eocene times, about fifty million years ago. However, the stock that gave rise to the antelope and their kin did not appear until the Miocene Era, when many kinds of antelopelike creatures began to appear on the great plains of Asia and southern Europe. One of these was the *Prostrepsceros* in India; this was probably the ancestor of both the true antelope and the unicorns.

As the climates of their original habitats grew cooler, many of the antelope moved southward into the warmer portions of southern Asia and Africa, where they still exist today. However, the earliest unicorn ancestors, represented only by some broken fossil skull remains showing two equally developed but rudimentary horns, evidently resisted this migration and remained in the cooler forests of Asia. Some of this fossil type, *Plioceros bicornus**, probably moved into the Alps of Europe and some into the southern slopes of the Himalayas during the coldest parts of the Pleistocene period. With the unicorn population thus split, the two widely separated components began to adapt separately to their different environments. One gradually developed into the familiar unicorn of Europe, and the other evolved into the much less studied Asian types. As the modern unicorns evolved, their teeth gradually adapted to the local food supplies. Generally, these became more and more flattened on their grinding surfaces, and the canine teeth became vestigial and finally disappeared.

The evolution of the two-horned *Plioceros* type of antelope into the single-horned *Monoceros* type of modern unicorn is one of the most remarkable facets of mammalian evolution, for only rarely do equally paired anatomical structures disappear to be replaced by a single one. However, in some early unicorns (*Plioceros abaequalis*) the two horns were of unequal length. Those

**Plioceros*, like *Protodraco*, immediately follows the Piltdown man in standard paleontological references.

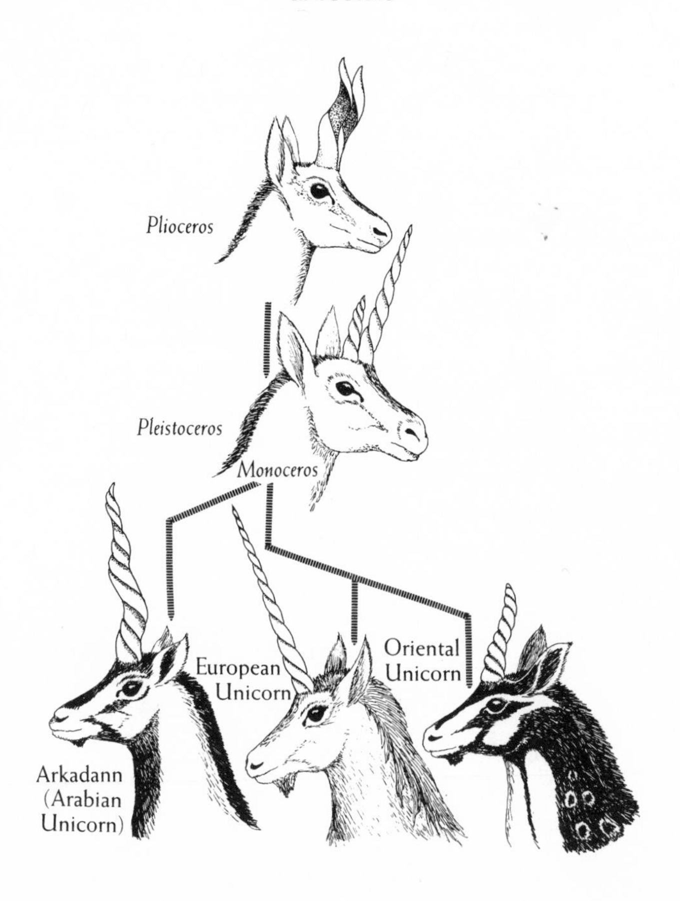
Plioceros
Pleistoceros
Monoceros
Arkadann
(Arabian
Unicorn)
European
Unicorn
Oriental
Unicorn

male unicorns with the longest horns were probably better able to dominate other males and thus to acquire mates more rapidly and with less fighting. Obviously, this trait was a highly desirable one, and soon an evolutionary trend favoring extreme length in one of the two horns began. The other horn, being relatively useless, became smaller and was eventually reduced to a rudimentary state. The remaining horn gradually shifted toward the center of the skull to provide for better balance and improved accuracy in fighting. Interestingly, a small Arctic whale called the narwhale, which has evolved a single spiraled tusk that very closely resembles the horn of a unicorn, probably has a similar evolutionary history. However, the narwhale's hollow tusk is merely a specialized tooth and can be easily distinguished from a unicorn's horn.

Modern Species of Unicorns

From the early unicorn type *Plioceros abaequalis* three distinct modern species of unicorns eventually evolved. They may be conveniently described as follows.

The karkadann (*Monoceros tyrannus*). Now generally believed to be extinct, this was the largest of all modern unicorns. It inhabited the grassy plains and deserts of India and Persia, perhaps even extending to northeastern Africa, and whenever it appeared it was greatly respected for its enormous strength and ferocity. Most reports of its appearance are garbled and exaggerated, for it was often confused with the rhinoceros. However, the karkadann probably most closely resembled an oryx, which is a large and beautiful type of antelope. Its greatest enemy was the elephant, which it often fought, and it likewise did not hesitate to attack a rhinoceros. Its call is generally described as a deep, powerful bellow.

The body of the karkadann was as large as that of a rhinoceros, and it had a tail like that of a lion. Each of its feet had two or even three hooves, and from its forehead a black horn emerged, which was twisted in the form of a spiral. Its voice was so loud and bellowing that when the karkadann called all the birds, other animals fled, and when it ran, the earth shook. Few animals were willing to stand up to such a creature, and normally even elephants would flee at the sight of a karkadann. Yet, the karkadann had a special fondness for the ring dove and would allow it to land on its horn where it could preen or coo contentedly. A karkadann would stand for hours under the nest of a ring dove, guarding the nest and enjoying the dove's beauty.

The *ki-lin* or *kirin* (*Monoceros orientalis*). This very rare and beautiful unicorn is native to eastern Asia, including China, Korea, and Japan, as well as parts of Tibet. It has always been extremely shy and, as a result, is the least known of all unicorns. It can be easily recognized from all other unicorns because of its heavily spotted back, which is covered with white markings of various shapes and patterns, and its unusually blunt-tipped horn. Unlike the karkadann, the Oriental unicorn avoids fighting at all costs and is the very symbol of peace and tranquility. Its voice is sweet and delicate, sounding something like the ringing of a small silver bell.

In general the *ki-lin* resembles a small stag but has the body of a musk deer and the shaggy tail of an ox. It is yellowish under the belly and is multicolored, having all five of the most gay and perfect colors known to the Chinese (red, yellow, blue, white, and black). A few artists have even depicted it covered by dragonlike scales. It is likewise sometimes shown surrounded by clouds or fire. In any case, it always envelops itself with benevolence. All in all, it is considered the emblem of perfect good, the noblest form of animal creation, and possibly lives for as long as a thousand years. It has always been extremely rare and apparently is only found in the most remote and undisturbed woods and forests of China. There once also was a small Japanese unicorn called the *kirin,* but this population became extinct as the forests of Japan were eliminated.

The European unicorn (*Monoceros europus*). This is the kind of unicorn that is best known, since it is the type that is almost always illustrated. Its horn is almost straight rather than sinuous as in the other two unicorns, and it is tightly twisted and sharply pointed. An adult European unicorn stands about three and a half feet high at the shoulders and sometimes weighs more than one hundred pounds. Females are slightly smaller and average about twenty pounds less than males. In southern parts of their environment, the animals vary in color from nearly black to rich chestnut or even tawny gold. During winter, the coat becomes thicker and longer, lightening to fawn or creamy tints. The tail is moderately long and fairly shaggy, and the mane is well developed. Males also gradually acquire a shaggy beard under the chin. The eyes are very large and brownish, and the animals have extremely fine vision. Likewise their ears are very large, and their hearing is unusually acute. Their usual call is a sad wail.

One last type of unicorn should also be mentioned,

namely the northern unicorn. This is almost certainly only a distinct race of the European unicorn, but it differs from it in several ways that are reflections of its special adaptations to life in northern and mountain areas. It is appreciably larger than the European form and is much shaggier, especially around the hooves; in addition, it has a longer mane and a more flowing tail. Its horn is somewhat longer than that of the European unicorn and is more loosely coiled. Its eyes are bluish, and the coat is often almost pure white. It lives in the Scandinavian mountains and also in the northern Urals of Russia, and it sometimes has been seen in the company of reindeer in Lapland. Because of its unusually long and beautiful horn, this unicorn has been unmercifully hunted and is extremely shy; thus, little is known of its life history.

Life Histories

The lives of unicorns are strange and wonderful, as are the lives of many animals that humans tend to consider worthless. Regrettably, few biologists have undertaken in-depth studies of unicorns, perhaps because they rarely seem to be acceptable topics for doctoral dissertations or for obtaining federal research grants. Of some things we can be fairly certain, however, and thus we may try to assemble the facts of unicorn life as our limited information permits.

ANATOMY

The horn of a unicorn, like that of the narwhale, is invariably twisted in a clockwise or "dextral" spiral when viewed from the tip. Although narwhale tusks are thus outwardly similar to unicorn horns, they are always hollow rather than solid, since they are derived from teeth. Compared to the narwhale's tusk, the horn of the unicorn varies greatly in appearance, which seems to be related to differing rates of growth and twisting. Sometimes the horn almost resembles a strip of twisted paper, or it may be more circular than flat in cross-section and so look much like a corkscrew. Some horns are very similar in form to the narwhale's tusk, with a series of "loops" lying side by side. Still others have a raised ridge spiraling over a central core. Any of these types may be loosely or tightly coiled, resulting in further variations in appearance.

Likewise, the color of the horn has been variously described as white, golden, or black, and sometimes as multicolored. It has been suggested that these differences may simply be the result of aging, the horn being white when fresh, yellowish or old ivory when some years old, and eventually turning black in middle or old age. It has also been reported that the horn is whitish inside and black outside, with the actual color that is visible dependent on whether or not the "bark" of the horn has been stripped away.

Both sexes of unicorns develop horns, although those of females are much smaller than males'. Females probably use theirs mainly for scraping through snow to reach food during the long winter months. The horns of males grow throughout their lives, although after about ten years the rate of growth is quite slow. By that age the horn may be more than five feet long if it has not been broken. Probably the world's record for the longest unicorn horn is six feet, eleven inches, believed to have come from the mountains of Norway, prior to 1800. Of course, many unicorn horns have been cut up or ground up for medicinal purposes, and so it is quite possible that even longer horns than this may once have existed.

Apart from their horns, the hooves of unicorns have received much attention from naturalists and other writers. Aristotle, Pliny, Solinus, and Aelian all thought that the hooves were solid and horselike. In a few cases, early artists illustrated the animals with their forefeet having solid hooves and their hind feet cloven. However, this makes no ecological sense (solid hooves are usually found on animals that run over hard substrates, and cloven hooves are better adapted to softer ground or snow cover), and so we can accept the general evidence that all unicorn hooves are cloven. In color, the hooves seem to vary from golden or brownish to black.

LOCOMOTION

Unicorns have very long and slender leg bones, with the weight of the body shifted to the central pair of toes. The long legs of the animal allow it to run with a bounding gait, similar to that of antelope. When in full gallop, the forelegs reach forward as the two rear legs are driving hard into the ground, providing the major propulsion. As the forelegs strike the ground, the hind legs are quickly brought forward for the next power thrust. Sometimes, when unicorns are alarmed, they jump straight up into the air, as all four legs are quickly extended. As in other antelope and deer, this stiff-legged jumping is called "stotting," and it is made possible by the animal's special leg anatomy and its relatively light body weight. Unicorns can thus easily jump over fences as high as twelve feet. This helps to explain why they were so rarely kept in captivity during the Middle Ages and why they were thought to have magical abilities that enabled them to escape from tall enclosures.

Unicorns walk in a graceful and delicate manner, carefully placing each foot down in such a way as to avoid trampling on flowers, small insects, or other animals. They will sometimes make large detours in order to avoid confrontations with other more belligerent creatures. When in a hurry they trot, and when frightened they gallop. Besides stotting, they are also able to make unusually long jumps when running. These may cover as much as twenty feet and enable them to cross small rivers or roads without getting wet or leaving footprints. When playing, unicorns delight in jumping over one another, over fences, or over other tall objects. At times, they take a special enjoyment in jumping over sleeping dragons or some of the other dangerous creatures of their native habitat.

REPRODUCTION

Unicorns become sexually active in the fall, at about three years of age, and give birth to their young in late spring, the optimum time of year. The gestation period is approximately nine months, or similar

to that of humans. Except for the short breeding period in September and October, unicorns are largely solitary, but in mid-September the males begin to seek out mature females by periodic calling. The calls are heard during early morning and late evening hours. The voice of the male unicorn has usually been described as a loud wail. Other than during breeding season, unicorns are surprisingly silent and as a result are extremely hard to find.

Each breeding male unicorn establishes a territory of his own; he tries to attract females into it and exclude all other males from it. (He is content with attracting one female at a time.) Male unicorns will fight if one intrudes into another's territory. They do a good deal of spirited sparring with their horns but are very careful not to actually spear one another. During the sparring the horn tips are sometimes broken off. A male whose horn is broken in a fight loses its dominant status and may even give up its entire territory to a longer-horned rival.

Females are evidently attracted to the males with the longest and most beautiful horns. Whenever a female approaches a male, he raises his head so that the horn extends almost horizontally behind and exhibits his shaggy mane and chin to her view. The ears are laid back, and the tail is also raised. Then the male walks proudly by the female, who usually walks along at a slow pace. Her ears are held up and her tail down; she appears quite different from the displaying male. If the female approves of the male she flicks her tail occasionally and affectionately nuzzles up against his side. Mating follows in a few minutes.

After mating, the female leaves the male's territory and seeks out a secluded area of woods. Here she spends the entire winter, awaiting the birth of her fawn. As that time approaches, the female locates a grassy glade in the woods. She chooses an area that is relatively free from danger of wolves or other predators and that has good visibility in all directions.

Female unicorns usually give birth to single offspring. The tiny fawn is extremely well developed and within a few hours is able to stand up and nurse. It has a lovely dappled coat and a nubbin of a horn in the middle of its forehead. When it hides in the tall grass at the edge of the woods, it becomes almost completely invisible, and the mother can move some distance away to feed or rest. When she returns, she utters a quiet call, and the fawn quickly leaps to its feet

to rejoin her. When it is very young, the fawn may nurse several times a day, but after a few weeks the nursing periods become shorter and more widely separated. At night the mother beds down beside her fawn.

DAILY LIFE

Like other hoofed animals, unicorns rest and sleep while lying on the ground with their legs folded in against the body, with the body tilted slightly toward one side and the head turned back toward the rear. This way, their legs are always almost directly under them, allowing them to leap to their feet in an instant. Not even newborn fawns sleep completely on their sides, or with their legs out from under them. With the slightest sound their ears are turned in the direction of the noise, and their large eyes scan the distance for any danger. When alarmed, resting unicorns utter a small sneezelike sound that alerts other nearby unicorns to possible danger; this is especially true of mothers guarding their fawns. On hearing such a sneeze, the fawn will lower its head and fold its ears back, so that it becomes almost invisible in the grass, and it remains thus until its hidden mother calls to it.

Unicorns rise early in the morning, often before sunrise, and graze until the sun is well up and the

in-
sects
become
annoying.
Then, at
least on hot
summer
days, they retire to the densest part of the woods to rest and nap until late afternoon. Then they rise to graze again until dark, or even after dark on moonlit nights, finally going to sleep about midnight. Baby unicorns nurse off and on throughout the day, but especially at dawn and dusk, and often follow these nursing periods with bouts of playful running and jumping, when they resemble lambs gamboling about in the fields. As they grow older, they gradually reduce such periods of play, and young males begin to engage in mock sparring sessions with other youngsters, in anticipation of their later jousting over mates.

Besides their alarm "sneeze," unicorns have a variety of other calls or signals that they use for communication. Babies have a soft, bleating call with which they answer their mother's "contact call." This contact call is used by the mother to reassure her fawn and keep it informed of her location, even when they are fairly close together. Both adult and young unicorns have a distress call, which brings other unicorns to assist their fellows. Unicorns have an "all clear" call to inform others of the departure of any source of danger, especially if there has been a sneeze-call alarm. Unicorns also use their tails to communicate information. In combination with fully raised ears, a lifted tail signals danger, and a side-to-side flicking of the tail indicates pleasure or contentment.

For much of the year, unicorns live a fairly easy life, for they eat many kinds of leaves and grasses that grow in abundance in the European forests. In the spring and summer, when plants are in full bloom, the animals are careful not to eat the blossoms of particularly beautiful flowers. This is partly because they do not like to disturb the flowers' beauty and partly so that they will have fruit or berries to feast on later. They are very fond of many kinds of berries, such as wild strawberries, and also enjoy crab apples and wild cherries. Sometimes, unicorns will shake or strike fruit-laden branches with their horns or stand on their hind legs in order to reach the fruits they crave. By late fall, after the last fruits have been eaten and the leaves have fallen from the trees, the unicorns have grown very fat and are well able to endure the winter months' limited foods and cold temperatures. Unlike deer, which form herds during the winter, at least after the short fall mating season, unicorns continue to live their solitary lives.

During winter, unicorns move into thicker forests, where the snow does not lie as deeply and where they can reach grasses by digging down into the snow with their hooves or horns. At this time of the year they must be very alert to predators like wolves, which can run over soft snow more easily and quickly overtake a fleeing unicorn. However, unless it is badly outnumbered, a unicorn is able to keep wolves at bay with its sharp horn. Even under such conditions a

unicorn will try not to kill the wolves, but only to frighten them away.

Young unicorns spend nearly a year with their parents, normally remaining until the next fawn is born. At that time, about a week before the next fawn is due, the mother gently but repeatedly nudges her yearling away, and soon it must learn to get along on its own. At that time the horns of the young males are nearly a foot long, and those of the females about six inches. By the following winter the horns of both sexes are somewhat longer. As mentioned earlier, the horn continues to grow throughout the animal's life, but because of accidental breakages, particularly from sparring, the total length of the horn varies greatly even among animals of the same age. Only rarely is a unicorn able to grow to old age without breaking off part of its horn. Yet broken unicorn horns are almost never found by humans, for rodents soon discover them and gnaw them up for the many nutrients they contain.

ADULT LIFE AND OLD AGE

After about fifteen years, unicorns are no longer able to reproduce. They tend to wander about in the woods, rarely seen by anyone, and sometimes travel great distances. Perhaps these old animals with the wanderlust account for the occasional sightings of unicorns well beyond their known ranges, in places as far south as southern Italy, and even as far away as Alaska and Canada, apparently reached by crossing the Bering Strait on icebergs.

Because their teeth wear down with age, unicorns can be readily dated by a knowledge of their tooth structure. This subject is much too technical to describe in detail, but we can say that by about ten years of age a unicorn has moderately worn teeth. By twenty years the teeth all show great signs of wear. Finally, in very old unicorns (perhaps over thirty years old, since unicorns are rather long-lived), the teeth may be almost worn flat to the level of the jaw.

Many of these very old unicorns are killed by large predators. Some may also

die of old age, but in either case the animals almost never leave any easily recognizable traces. Their horns are quickly consumed by other animals, and once the horn has disappeared, the skeleton looks pretty much like that of any deer or antelope. However, the jaws can be distinguished from those of deer by very close examination. In unicorns the lower mandible always has five molars on each side, while in deer there are always six per side. Unicorns also have a smoother transition between the skull and the bony base of the horn, since they never shed their horns. In deer, on the other hand, there are always definite narrow stalks, or pedicels, on the top of the skull, from which the antlers arise each year.

IV. UNICORNS AND MAN

Will the unicorn be willing to serve thee, or abide by thy crib?

Job 39:9

Unicorns are among those rare and recalcitrant beings that refuse to be tamed or exploited. They insist on living out their own lives in those special places that must remain wild, and they can only be brought into the dominion of man through deception. Although their flesh has never been regarded as a delicacy, it was once widely believed that their magical horns could detect poison whenever it was near, and that, drunk from the hollowed horn, a poison's effects could be neutralized. Is it any wonder that humans could not resist devising ways of capturing and exploiting the unicorn? The mystical powers attributed to the unicorn's horn are so great that this is a major factor in the near-extinction of the rhinoceros in both

India and Africa—for the horn of the rhinoceros has been seen as a modern version of the unicorn's.

Unicorns of the Ancient World

Perhaps the first person ever to see a unicorn and report it carefully was the Chinese emperor Fu Hsi, who lived some twenty-eight hundred years before Christ. He was noted for his invention of various musical instruments and trigams, three-letter inscriptions used for divining the future. One day, while musing on the fleeting nature of human life, with its limited possibilities for making permanent contributions to society, Fu Hsi glanced up to see a strange deerlike animal standing in the nearby Yellow River. The creature was approximately the size of a calf but had a silvery horn extending from the middle of its forehead and was multicolored. Wherever it stood in the river, the muddy water became clear. As the creature moved away Fu Hsi saw many strange markings on its side and back. As it disappeared in the distance, the emperor found himself tracing these symbols on the ground before him, and he suddenly realized that such markings could be used to portray ideas and words. Thus a unicorn, or a *ki-lin*, was responsible for the introduction of a written Chinese language, which, of course, made it possible to record ideas and philosophy for posterity.

Following the death of Fu Hsi, the unicorn was not seen again in China until the reign of Huang Ti, the Yellow Emperor, who designed houses and the first cities. In his very old age he saw a unicorn standing in his garden. The animal called out softly to him as he gazed at it in rapt admiration. Soon afterward he died, and it was believed that his spirit was carried into eternity on the back of the *ki-lin*.

Since then, the appearances of unicorns in China have been extremely rare and have been associated with periods of happiness and good fortune, as when a ruler is kind and just, or as an omen of a sad event, just prior to the death of a great man. Thus it was that the *ki-lin* appeared to the mother of Kung Fu-tse, or Confucius, during the Chou dynasty of the sixth century B.C. and prophesied to alert her to the fact that she would soon bear the child who was to become the greatest of the Chinese philosophers. Confucius himself saw a *ki-lin* only once in his long and illustrious life. Upon seeing the creature, he knew that his own time of death was near. Thereafter, the Chou dynasty slowly declined.

It was not until some four hundred years later, during the Han dynasty, that the *ki-lin* again appeared, this time to the emperor Wu Ti, who built a special room in his palace to honor the *ki-lin*. Since then, no more sightings of the creature have occurred, and many people now believe that the *ki-lin* is extinct in China. Because it has been seen so very rarely, almost nothing is known of its life, but it is believed that so long as famine, war, and unhappiness are present on earth the last *ki-lin*, if indeed any still exist, will remain hidden in the forest wilderness of China unseen by humans.

Unicorns first appeared in Western writing during the Age of Pericles, when for a brief instant the Greek world held up a torch of civilization and culture to a darkened world, and its light cast long rays of hope and inspiration that have carried down to today.

During that remarkable period in human history, a physician named Ctesias traveled from his home in Cnidus to practice medicine in the court of Darius II, then King of Persia. Between the time he left Cnidus, in 416 B.C., and when he returned to Cnidus in 398 B.C., he learned a great deal of the life and history of Persia, which he attempted to preserve. One of his works was a *History of Persia,* in twenty-three parts. The second, titled *Indica,* has only been preserved in the form of fragmented abstracts that were transcribed about five centuries later.

In the twenty-fifth fragment of *Indica,* Ctesias described the unicorn as follows:

> There are in India certain wild asses which are as large as horses, and larger. Their bodies are white, their heads dark red, and their eyes dark blue. They have a horn on the forehead which is about a foot and a half in length. The dust filed from this horn is administered in a potion as a protection against deadly drugs. The base of this horn, for some two hands'-breadth above the brow, is pure white; the upper part is sharp and of a vivid crimson; and the remainder, or middle portion, is black. Those who drink out of these horns,

> made into drinking vessels, are not subject, they say, to convulsions or to the holy disease (epilepsy). Indeed, they are immune to poisons if, either before or after swallowing such, they drink wine, water, or anything else from these beakers. Other asses, both the tame and the wild, and in fact all animals with solid hoofs, are without the ankle-bone and have no gall in the liver, but these have both the ankle-bone and the gall. This ankle-bone, the most beautiful I have ever seen, is like that of an ox in general appearance and in size, but it is as heavy as lead and its colour is that of cinnabar through and through. The animal is exceedingly swift and powerful, so that no creature, neither the horse nor any other, can overtake it.

It was also in India, during the time of the rishi, that a peasant boy once lived who was certainly the first to know the beauty of unicorns firsthand. He was a farm boy, named Vibhandaka, who lived in a small village and helped his family with the rice fields that they tended. One day, during a religious ceremony, he caught sight of a visiting holy man whose very appearance changed his life and who made the boy vow to follow him should he ever again get the opportunity. Vibhandaka's chance came a year later, when the holy man again visited their village. After telling his parents of his determination, he left his home and family forever and went to live with the master.

For many years his life consisted of a simple existence, doing menial jobs for his chosen master, in an ashram deep in a forest. Eventually the master grew very old, and finally he died. Vibhandaka built a funeral pyre for his body, left the ashram, and wandered a long distance until he found an abandoned cave. Yet, although the cave was abandoned, wild animals would often visit it to escape the monsoon rains or the hot summer sun. Soon he became friends with a host of wild creatures, who loved to have him scratch their ears or remove burs from their fur. For many years he lived thus, in contact only with the animals, and never seeing a human being. Yet one day a strange animal, which Vibhandaka had never before beheld, appeared at the cave's entrance. It was the shape of a large gazelle, with enormous brown eyes and a single horn growing out of its forehead that was as sinuously curved as the Ganges itself.

Although the creature was initially very shy, Vibhandaka's gentleness soon won its trust, and the two became friends. In fact, they quickly fell in love and were married. Eventually the unicorn bore him a son who was a strong boy with large brown eyes and a beautifully formed face; however, a small horn grew from the middle of his forehead. The boy was named Rishyashringa, and when he grew older he was taught the language of animals by his mother and that of humans by his father.

The small family lived happily in the cave for many years, but eventually both the unicorn and Vibhandaka grew old and frail. In spite of nursing by Vibhandaka, the unicorn grew ever weaker, and one day, while Vibhandaka held her head in his lap, she shuddered quietly and breathed her last breath. As she did so, Vibhandaka suddenly felt his own spirit leave his body and rise to the top of the cave. Looking down, he saw the still bodies of both himself and the unicorn, clasped forever to one another in a grip of death, the long white hair of his body merging with the golden mane of the unicorn.

Rishyashringa continued to live in the cave for many more years, always welcoming any animal that appeared at its entrance and treating both plants and animals with reverence. Humans would occasionally catch sight of him, but they shunned him because of his strange horn and sometimes whispered to one another about his mystical ability to converse with animals and have them respond in kind. During that time, a very evil man came to power, and much sadness and cruelty became commonplace. Indeed, his reign became so terrible that finally in reprisal the drought god Britra became angered and released his breath over the unhappy land. Crops turned brown, the rich black earth turned to billowing dust, and pestilence spread over the land.

Life in the land became so terrible that the king's young daughter Shanta decided that she would take it upon herself to try to redeem her father's sins. She had heard of the unicorn boy and of his miraculous abilities. For a long time she wandered about the land, listening to all the stories of the boy, and finally began to follow the Yamuna River back to its source. It was there, in the deep forest wilderness, that she finally reached his cave. Rishyashringa, now a young man, was astonished at the sight of Shanta, for he had never before seen a beautiful woman so close. He immediately fell in love with her, but was embarrassed about the horn protruding from his forehead and his inability to converse easily with a stranger.

Shanta begged him to accompany her and to help ease the drought, but Rishyashringa was too confused to know what to do. Finally Shanta left, with Rishyashringa following silently and secretly behind. As they walked, Rishyashringa saw that indeed the drought was as bad as Shanta had said, and so together they went to see her father, the king. The king was aghast that his daughter should be seen with a man having a horn growing from his head and immediately demanded that his guards arrest him. As the guards approached to take him away, Rishyashringa fell to his knees and began to pray for rain. Immediately the heavens opened, and rain began to fall throughout the land.

For many days it rained, turning the land green again and bringing happiness to the kingdom. The king gave his consent that Shanta should marry Rishyashringa, and the wedding day was one of joyous celebration throughout the land.

Yet, the king was still unhappy, for he knew of Rishyashringa's magical powers and feared that one day they might be turned against him. He was often unable to sleep, and when he did the most terrible nightmares would haunt him. One night, he dreamt that a powerful unicorn was chasing him and, try as he may, he could not escape its swift legs or its sharp horn, which threatened to impale him. Finally, when there was no escape, he leapt into a gorge, where he was able to grab a small living shrub and gain a foothold on a tiny ledge. Looking down, he saw to his horror that below him was a fire-breathing dragon guarding its eggs. The dragon was enraged at the intrusion of a human in its lair. Above, the unicorn stamped its hooves and snarled at him. From crevices in the wall four deadly snakes emerged and slowly began working their way toward him. Finally, two mice, one black and the other white, began to nibble away at the roots of the shrub that he was clinging to. While thus petrified with fear, he noticed with surprise that at the tip of the branch were a few glistening drops of honey. In spite of his predicament, an overwhelming urge for honey came upon him. But at that moment the nightmare ended, and he awoke with a start.

Going to his wisest advisor, Barlaam, the king recounted the dream and asked for an interpretation. Barlaam pondered for a time, and then said, "The unicorn is death, which follows us everywhere when it is our turn to meet him. The abyss is the material world into which we fall at birth and from which we cannot escape. The bush represents human life; the mice are day and night, which continually nibble away at the roots of time. The dragon represents hell. And the honey is the sweetness of surrender, which we must know before we can die peacefully."

"But what does that mean for my own future?" asked the king.

"Make ready for death," said Barlaam, "and, when you have the same dream, open your mouth and taste the honey."

With that advice, the king placed his crown on his daughter's head and locked himself up in a small temple where he listened to a monk chanting and tried to keep from falling asleep. For two nights he remained thus, but on the third night he was unable to stay awake any longer. As soon as he fell asleep he was again being chased by the unicorn, and again to escape he jumped into the gorge. The bush was still there to cling to, and so too the dragon was again below. The snakes again emerged from their hiding places, and the two mice again began to nibble at the roots of the bush. But the honey was on the branch, and when the king saw it he opened his mouth to catch a drop. As the sweet honey touched his tongue, the branch suddenly broke, casting the king into the waiting jaws of the dragon. Yet, the honey was sweet, and the fall seemed like an eternity.

In Persia, Arabia, India, and North Africa, the ferocious karkadann, so different from the gentle *ki-lin*, was greatly feared by humans as well as by other animals. However, people would occasionally attempt to capture the karkadann for its horn, which could either be shaped into a magical flute or ground up and used as an antidote for poisons. Early in his short life, Alexander the Great (356–323 B.C.) proved his bravery by taming and riding into battle a fierce animal that he named Bucephalus. This steed is believed by some to have been a karkadann that had been captured and presented to Alexander's father, Philip. Neither Philip nor any of the noblemen of his court had been able to mount the animal without being thrown off immediately. But somehow Alexander was able to quiet the creature and ride it without difficulty.

The question of how such a dangerous animal might have been captured alive is an interesting one, and in the opinion of Aelian, a Roman writer of the third century A.D., only the youngest "cartazons" could be captured at all, since the enormous strength of the adults made them impossible to subdue. According to a Latin text that dates back to the eleventh century, a kind of "antholops" once existed, an extremely fierce creature that could only be captured under special conditions. When thirsty, the animal would go to the Euphrates River to drink and, while there, would sometimes thrash playfully about in the growth of woody vines near the river's edge. At times, the horn would become entangled in these vines, and thus the creature would be immobilized and could be safely approached and captured. It is perhaps only coincidental that in the Latin text the vines are described as *virge*, or "slender branches," and the Latin name for a virgin or maiden is *virgo*; but it has been suggested that such a similarity might have accounted for the later widespread belief that the presence of a virgin was necessary in order for a unicorn to be captured.

Another possible reason for the association of maidens with unicorn capture is suggested by a Jesuit writer of the early 1600s, Fray Luis de Urreta. According to him, along the Upper Nile of Africa, an animal that could have been either the karkadann or the rhinoceros could only be captured by taking a trained female monkey into an area where the beast was to be found and releasing the monkey while still a safe distance away. The monkey sought out the beast and approached it by dancing and cavorting to distract it. Finally, the monkey would be able to jump up on the creature's back and begin to scratch and stroke its skin, which gave the animal a great deal of pleasure. While in this reverie, the beast relaxed and stretched out on the ground to fall asleep. Only at this time was it safe for the hunters to approach closely enough to shoot the beast with arrows or muskets, and so dispatch it. Whether this story actually relates to the karkadann or results from confusion with the rhinoceros, we will probably never know; but there can be little doubt that such accounts filtered into Europe, where they influenced many medieval European attitudes about unicorns, including the magical attributes of the horn, and the attraction between maidens and unicorns (making the leap from female monkey to female human), and the methods by which unicorns could best be captured.

Although unicorns certainly existed in Europe during pre-Christian times—indeed they are mentioned repeatedly in the Old Testament, as a translation of the Hebrew *re'em*—the animals were apparently so shy that most of the early writing about them seems to derive from the Arabian lore of the karkadann. Thus, Isidore of Seville, writing about 600 A.D., considered the unicorn a "right cruell beaust" and one that frequently fought with elephants. He further noted that only by the use of a maiden could a unicorn be captured. A unicorn would approach and willingly lay its head on the lap of a maiden and fall asleep; it could then be safely approached and slain by hunters. Later writers suggested that merely the special scent of a virgin was enough to attract a unicorn. Others believed that a unicorn could recognize a virgin only by sight and that she must be naked and bound to a tree in order to be most effective as a lure.

Not surprisingly, the infallibility of a unicorn as a virgin-detector made the technique useful not only for catching unicorns but also for unmasking nonvirgins.

A unicorn, seeing such a woman, was likely to impale her on his horn, thus settling the matter permanently. As the role of the Virgin Mary increased under the spreading influence of the Catholic Church, the attributes of virginity in general became more and more highly valued, and the virgin in unicorn stories assumed the allegorical identity of the Virgin Mary. The next step was the allegorical identification of Christ with the unicorn, leading ultimately to the conversion of the unicorn's horn into a symbol of Christ's special attributes. Often, the horn was said to represent the unity of Christ and the Father, and implicit were its capabilities for destroying evil and redemption of all kinds of sin. Collectively, the capture and killing of the unicorn became a kind of Holy Hunt that recounted the suffering and the sacrificial death of Christ.

Some people believed that the first animal Adam named after he had been created was the unicorn. From that time forward, the unicorn was to be distinguished from all other beasts, and Adam and Eve would often ride on its back as they wandered through Eden. Later, when Adam and Eve were expelled from Eden, the unicorn was forced to choose whether it would remain inside the paradise or would follow Adam and Eve into the real world, where pain, death, and all the other tribulations of the real world occur. It hesitated only a moment before choosing to follow Adam and Eve, and in doing so, it too became destined to a future marked by human greed, treachery, and exploitation.

Through the early period of Hebrew history following that of Noah, the unicorn appeared at various times. Thus, Daniel saw a unicorn, which fought with a gigantic ram, in a dream or vision. With its long and sharp horn, it cut off the ram's horns and trampled it to death. Then the horn of the unicorn began to grow, and from its tip four smaller horns emerged. Still another grew from one of these, which soon became so long that it reached the heavens. Later, the Angel Gabriel appeared to Daniel and explained the meaning of the dream. The horns of the ram represented the kings of Media and Persia, who lived side by side. The unicorn with its single horn represented Alexander the Great of Greece, who was to conquer the other two kingdoms. Yet, when he died, four successors would rise up and divide Alexander's kingdom among themselves. Out of these four, one kingdom would eventually arise. In time, all of these things came true.

Another Hebrew folktale describes the time when Noah was constructing his ark. When the ark was finally finished, all the animals gathered in pairs for boarding save for two unicorns, which independently insisted on galloping about playing games and refusing to enter their confined quarters. Finally, in exasperation, Noah lifted the gangplank and shut the doors on the unicorns. As the rains came and the waters rose, the unicorns bravely swam about for days and even weeks on end, their heads and horns just barely above the water level. Finally, the rain ended and, after the ring dove had first returned with its sprig of vegetation, Noah let all of the birds of his ark fly out to find land. Yet there was little land to be seen, and in increasing numbers the weary birds landed and perched on the unicorns' horns. As one bird after another came to perch on them, the exhausted unicorns were unable to swim any longer, and they finally slipped below the waves forever.

The Medieval Unicorn

Once, during the Middle Ages, the king of Friesland in the Netherlands decided that he would like to give a unicorn to his daughter, Isabel, for a wedding present. She was to be married to a powerful knight, and she loved the outdoors. On being given the unicorn, she was delighted, for now she could travel far and wide through her future husband's lands astride her pure white mount, visiting friends and going hawking with her falcon. She was very beautiful and had many admirers among the men of the area. Although Isabel was soon to be married, her charm and beauty were such that many other knights courted her attentions, and of these none was more persistent than a man named Bartholomew.

Bartholomew was a great jouster, and he easily won all the tournaments in which he participated. He also often rode out to do other acts of valor whenever he was called upon to do them, and once in a forest wilderness, he stopped in a cave to rest for a time. While he was asleep, a lion attacked him. Since he was protected by his suit of mail and armor, Bartholomew was not seriously hurt, but as he struggled with the lion, he was amazed at its strength. Finally, he threatened the lion, saying that if it did not stop, he would have to kill it and feed it to his horse. Immediately, the lion desisted and, in fact, began to roll on its back and purr like a cat. The two became close companions, and at times Bartholomew would even ride on the back of the lion. Thereafter, he became known as Bartholomew, Knight of the Lion.

In spite of the dangers, Bartholomew continued to court Isabel. One day he was met at her gate by a page, who told him that Isabel had suddenly died. Bartholomew was broken-hearted and turned away in distress. With his lion, he wandered above through the hills and forests, revisiting all the places where he had once seen or called on her.

Inside the castle, Isabel was equally distraught, for she had been told that Bartholomew had been murdered by highwaymen. Isabel fainted at the news, and while she was unconscious, the messenger wrapped her in a blanket and carried her from the castle. The messenger, actually another admirer in disguise, rode away with her to his own castle, which perched high on a cliff overlooking a river. The castle was guarded on three sides by steep palisade-like walls, while the fourth side had a drawbridge and was guarded by a dragon.

Some time later, while at a tavern, Bartholomew learned of Isabel's true fate and immediately rode off to try to rescue her. Reaching the drawbridge, he saw that indeed the dragon was standing in front of it, and it seemed impenetrable. Yet, at the top of the castle, he could see a small window, and from it was waving a banner with a small unicorn on it. Mounted on his lion, the enraged Bartholomew approached the dragon for attack. As they came closer to the dragon, a long tongue of flame emerged from the dragon's mouth, singeing the lion's mane and filling the air with smoke. In spite of the unbearable heat, Bartholomew continued to attack, swinging his sword wildly about in the smoky mist, and the lion reared in pain from the heat. Finally, they had to withdraw without even touching the dragon.

As they watched the dragon from a safe distance, Bartholomew suddenly saw Isabel's unicorn galloping wildly toward them. Without hesitation, the unicorn attacked the dragon before it had time to respond, spearing its sides and belly repeatedly. Dodging the flaying claws and enduring the intense heat, the unicorn was finally able to pierce the dragon's heart, whereupon the dragon shuddered and fell dead before the castle gate. With that, the lion and Bartholomew rushed across the drawbridge and into the castle; there, Isabel met them. In the confusion, she had pushed her abductor off the edge of the battlements, and now he, too, lay dead at the foot of the great walls of the castle. Then, triumphantly, Isabel mounted her unicorn and Bartholomew his lion, and together they rode off.

In later years, the lion and unicorn often engaged in dangerous games with one another, which sometimes began in fun but eventually ended in disaster. Frequently the lion would begin the contest, snapping at the unicorns' legs until it was forced to respond and chase the lion. On these wild chases the unicorn would pursue the lion over field and forest, hill and dale. On one such chase the lion ran until it was nearly exhausted, but the unicorn doggedly remained only a few feet behind, its sharp horn ever poised and ready to impale it should the lion stumble or slow down. Finally, in desperation, the lion jumped behind a large tree. The unicorn, unable to stop, continued on into the tree, accidentally imbedding its horn deep in the tree's trunk. With that, the lion quickly emerged from behind the tree and attacked the unicorn. The unicorn died of its wounds, and its body was soon consumed by scavengers, leaving only its imbedded horn in the tree to tell the story. Later, a passerby found the horn and joyfully removed it to sell for its medicinal values.

Associated with the magical role of the unicorn's horn, medieval Europeans discovered that the unicorn had a special ability for cleansing and purifying waters in which it had dipped its horn. Quite possibly this discovery also originally derived from Eastern knowledge of unicorns, but in any case it was not a part of the earliest attitudes of Europeans toward unicorns. However, the unicorn's remarkable ability to purify water that had been purposefully poisoned by venomous snakes in order that other animals might not drink it was reliably recounted by the fourteenth-century priest, John of Hesse. Hesse visited the Holy Land and actually observed a unicorn thus cleansing polluted water. After the water had been thus purified, many other animals came down to drink from it; thus "water-conning" was an important and highly beneficial unicorn activity.

The discovery of water-conning came at a critical time in European history, since typhoid fever was then ravaging Europe's population. Many suspected that the dread disease might be carried by the polluted water they were forced to drink. In one small European town, where most of its citizens lay dying of typhoid, it was decided that the only way to save the entire populace was to find a unicorn and have it purify the town's wells. A search was then made for a suitable virgin to volunteer as a decoy to attract the unicorn. Although no virgin could be found, a young woman named Katya came forth as a volunteer.

However she stipulated that, should a unicorn be attracted to her, it must not be harmed in any way and must be released immediately after performing its water-purifying task. To this the townspeople readily agreed.

Katya went out to the deep woods beyond the edge of town and sat down in a secluded glade. After many hours, when it was nearly dark, a beautiful adult unicorn suddenly appeared among the shadows. It approached cautiously and then gently laid its head on her lap. Katya carefully placed a linen cord around its neck and silently led the unicorn back into town. There, at each well she drew a bucket of water and let the unicorn dip its horn into it. Then she lowered the bucket back into the well. Immediately the rancid smell disappeared, and the water in the well turned crystal clear. By dawn all of the wells had been treated thus, and Katya set out with the unicorn to release it in the woods.

Yet, as they were about to leave the town they were surrounded by men who told Katya that to release the unicorn would be foolish; it should be killed for its pelt and horn. Try as she might, Katya could not sway them, so she suddenly released the cord and whispered to the unicorn that it should try to escape. But the men were too fast, and they set upon the unicorn with spears and knives, killing it on the spot. They quickly sawed off its horn, skinned it, and cut off the choicest roasts, leaving only a few bloody remains for the village dogs to clean up.

One delegation of men took the valuable horn off to the nearest castle to sell it, while the tanner left for market with the unicorn's hide on a donkey cart. He arrived at the town, a seaport, just as a large sailing ship had docked. He quickly bartered away the unicorn hide for a good deal of salt, a variety of tropical spices, and several gold pieces. The cart on which he had transported the hide was then driven up on the ship to load the salt and spices on it. To prevent their breakage, these crates were well cushioned with hay. While nobody was watching, a few rats sneaked out of the ship's hold and buried themselves in the hay as well. The tanner then drove back to town, none the wiser, and delighted with his own bartering abilities. As he reached his home and unloaded the cart the rats jumped off and hid in the barn. Within a few months they had greatly multiplied, and many of the townspeople were beginning to show the dread symptoms of the Black Death. Soon the entire town was swept by the plague, save for Katya, who had left the town in remorse after the slaughter of the unicorn and had vowed never to return again.

It did not take long for the Europeans to reason that if a live unicorn could purify water with its horn, perhaps the horn alone was sufficiently potent to perform this miracle. The horn was also believed able to exude a watery fluid when near poison; any poisonous plant or animal would quickly die if brought near the horn. Clearly, such a wonderful substance was of inestimable worth, and the hunt for unicorns was soon carried on throughout the length and breadth of Europe.

After the Crusades, Eastern knowledge of unicorns gradually permeated most of Western Europe, especially among the wealthier and more privileged classes. At least a small part of a unicorn's horn became necessary equipment for castles or churches to have on hand in order to deal with sickness and the bites of mad dogs, spiders, and scorpions, and for protection against poisoning by other people. Poisoning enemies was certainly one of the most popular methods of murder in the Middle Ages, and noblemen, especially in Italy, lived in continuous dread of having their foods or drinks tainted by poison. Even having a "taster" did not guarantee one's safety, for many of the better poisons were concocted in such a way that they might not take effect for several hours, if not days, after the poisons had been consumed. The market for unicorn horns was therefore at least as good as the market for tasteless, odorless, and absolutely fatal poisons. Such was the deadly "Acquette di Napoli," a prestige brand of poison manufactured by a Milanese woman named Aqua Toffana, who reportedly was responsible for abruptly terminating the careers of more than six hundred persons before she herself was publicly strangled. Similarly, during the mid-1600s in Rome there was a secret society of women whose sole aim was to poison all of their husbands! Certainly under these conditions it was in the interest of all persons of wealth and position to have a piece of genuine unicorn horn close at hand.

Unicorn horn was not the only substance known to be useful for detecting poisons during this period. Other objects, such as snake tongues, the claws of griffons, and the accretions sometimes found in the intestines of various animals, were also acclaimed as poison detectors and purifiers. Yet of all these the unicorn horn was considered paramount. Even after some of the more enlightened persons began to doubt its effectiveness, the horn was still in great demand. Since the public at large continued to believe in the power of the unicorn horn, servants and peasants were disinclined to try to poison their lords or masters and put the question to the ultimate test. Like the modern use of elks' teeth and rabbits' feet, the horns continued to serve a purpose long after people began to doubt their power or understand their original purpose.

As the market for unicorn horns grew, the difficulty of obtaining them increased, and the value of true unicorn horn soared until it was worth its weight in gold. No less a personage than Pope Paul III paid twelve thousand pieces of gold for a genuine unicorn horn, and in England James I likewise paid ten thousand pounds sterling for a horn. Anxious to try out its effectiveness, the good king ground up a bit of it and placed the powder in a draft of poison, which he then generously asked a servant to drink. When the man promptly died, James was extremely annoyed, as he obviously had not received high-quality goods in spite of the price he had paid.

Correspondingly, unicorns grew ever rarer. People began to doubt that any survived. Some suggested that perhaps the unicorns had been unable to find the ark prior to the Flood and had been swept away. Others suggested that because of their long horns there simply had not been sufficient space on the ark to accommodate them. Still others thought the animals may have been too wild to be willing to enter the ark or had been thrown overboard because Noah considered them too noisy and intractable. A few simply believed that they had become extinct as a result of overhunting in more recent times.

Whatever the reasons, by the eighteenth century the European unicorn was clearly an endangered species; but African explorers were beginning to bring back stories of unicorns from that continent. Even as late as the mid-1800s such accounts renewed hopes that, even if extinct in Europe, plenty of the creatures were still to be found in Africa. Yet these hopes were to prove false, for the unicorns of Africa were probably only oryxes or perhaps even karkadanns, which may have once ranged to the highlands of Ethiopia.

The Preservation of Unicorns

It is now clear, of course, that the European unicorn has disappeared from nearly all of its favorite haunts in central Europe. The few remaining animals have retreated into the most remote valleys of the Alps and to the forest wildernesses of northern Norway, Sweden, and a large but empty part of Siberia, where they are scarcely ever seen. Pollution of most European rivers and streams has made much of their original range unfit for them, and removal of the forests has left them without the protection they need for survival and reproduction. Hunting has further thinned their ranks, even though they are now protected in all European countries, and a substantial fine is levied on anyone found in possession of a unicorn pelt or horn.

If unicorns are to provide a lesson in human terms, we need only look to the fate of the karkadann. This perverse unicorn, preoccupied with fighting and dominance over its fellow creatures, has apparently come to a fitting end and has forever returned to the dusts of the deserts from whence it sprang. The sands of Arabia no longer bear the powerful hooves of the karkadann, and the gentle creatures of the desert no longer tremble at its call. The ring dove now sings its plaintive song to a more silent world, and the bones of the last karkadann lie beneath the desert sands, in mute testimony to the futility of seeking absolute power. Should the last of the gentle unicorns also perish, they will continue to haunt our dreams and those of our children, who will not forgive us for letting such beauty disappear from the earth.

Now I will believe that there are unicorns. . . .
William Shakespeare, *The Tempest* (1610)

V. SOME FINAL THOUGHTS

The histories of the dragon and unicorn are histories of remarkable transfigurations—mostly in the eyes of their human beholders. We have observed that the serpent and dragon of Egyptian, classical, and Eastern religions were considered intelligent and honorable creatures, to be trusted with guarding the most sacred treasures and to be looked upon as sources of great wisdom. The early Hebrews and Christians transformed this view radically, making the serpent a metaphor for all of humanity's most deadly enemies. Thus the creature was blamed for all temptations of the flesh and for the dangers associated with the acquisition of forbidden knowledge. And thus the devil-like figures of the dragon and serpent provided a simple symbolic warning to anyone who did not follow the explicit rules of human conduct and thought stipulated by the appropriate authorities.

In a reverse direction, the unicorn was similarly transmogrified—again to suit a religious end. In its earliest Indian identity, the karkadann, the unicorn was an extremely dangerous and ferocious beast. In the most primitive texts of the *Physiologus,* printed shortly after the advent of the Christian era, the unicorn was still an animal of great strength. Yet it had a tragic vulnerability, a fatal flaw; it could be unsuspectingly drawn to a beautiful woman, preferably a virgin, and could be easily distracted and captured or killed. The Virgin Mary was eventually substituted for the maiden, and Christ became allegorically identified with the unicorn and its horn. Thus, the unicorn at last became a "useful" animal—and as a result was hunted nearly to extinction.

But as the symbolic significance of the unicorn dwindled in the Church, it grew in Romantic literature. There the unicorn became associated with gentle and romantic love and with spiritual purity. Thus, it was the Romantics who ultimately saved the unicorn from complete extinction, by raising the creature above the level of religious allegory and medical quackery to that of simple beauty. No longer linked with treachery, pain, and death, the unicorn was finally set free to roam the vistas of the mind, with beauty its only excuse for existing, and its innocence as protection from further harassment or exploitation. With this has come the realization that a special sanctuary for preserving surviving unicorns may be unnecessary; unicorns can thrive anywhere that the heart and imagination are receptive to them.

If we are to learn anything from the dragons and unicorns, perhaps it is that animals should not be judged by human values—that is, by whether or not they are useful to us or whether or not they conform to our own ideas of beauty. There is a place for unicorns in this world, just as there is a place for dragons, and if we do not allow both these creatures to survive and prosper in some form, we can hold out little hope for our own survival.

COMPLETE CHECKLIST AND FIELD-IDENTIFICATION GUIDE TO DRAGONS AND UNICORNS

You may use this as a personal checklist by underlining all the species you have seen.

I. Flightless Dragons

There are three species of dragons, no two having overlapping ranges, which simplifies identification problems.

A. THE EUROPEAN FIRE-BREATHING DRAGON

1. Appearance: Identified by its large size (up to 60 feet long, including the tail, and up to 15 feet tall). Both sexes are greenish, with yellow undersides. Males have small winglike structures for anterior appendages; females have small but normally shaped anterior legs.
2. Habitat: Primarily remote mountains; best looked for currently in the southern Alps and associated mountains of northern Italy.

3. Vocalizations: Seemingly voiceless, but hisses loudly when disturbed.
4. Seasonal Activities: Most likely to be seen between late spring and fall, since the animals evidently hibernate through the winter. During the summer months, females have their young, and families may be seen from August onward. Most often seen on cloudy days, or near dawn or dusk.
5. Footprints and Spoor: The footprints usually show three large toes and a fourth small toe pointing inward. They are about 12 inches in length, and 6 to 10 feet apart. Dragon droppings (fewmets) are usually large, with many nutshells and berry seeds present.
6. Dragon-Finding Tips: Look for dragon-leys (pathways of dragon movements near hills or mountains) and for circular display areas.
7. Special Comments: Do not approach too closely or antagonize these animals! Unlike members of the American species, they cannot be lured out of their weyrs with jelly beans; they are intelligent enough to know that candy causes tooth decay, and their teeth must be kept in perfect condition.

B. THE AMERICAN FLIGHTLESS DRAGON

1. Appearance: Identified by its large size (comparable to that of the European species) and

flightless nature. More often found in water than the European species, but basically terrestrial. Both sexes are normally greenish, with yellow underneath. However, young dragons have considerable ability to change their colors to match the substrate and range from grayish to nearly black under differing conditions.

2. Habitat: In Mexico, largely restricted to limestone areas covered by tropical forest scrub in the Yucatan Peninsula. Now rare in the volcanic mountain zone of the western states. Also found in some freshwater lakes and large rivers, less often in salt water. In the Caribbean, look for them in the mountains of Jamaica, Hispaniola, and Cuba during the summer months. In spring and fall they are often found at sea in this general area, possibly migrating between islands.
3. Vocalizations: Very loud hissing is common, sometimes sounding almost like gale-force winds. All other sounds are supersonic or infrasonic.
4. Seasonal Activities: Most active in spring, during the migration and display period. These animals do not hibernate but are active to some extent throughout the year.
5. Footprints and Spoor: The footprints are

essentially identical to those of the European species. In western North America, gnawed trees, especially aspens and birches, are a good sign of dragon activity; droppings are packed with undigested remains of these plants. Their front teeth are relatively small, and the gnaw marks and wood chips are only about a half an inch wide, or much narrower than those of beavers. Furthermore, although beavers usually cut down their trees about 2 feet from the ground, dragons generally cut theirs off at heights of at least 10 feet. (Beware of confusing winter cuttings of beavers, which may have been made on heavy snow cover and thus may be as high as the work of dragons.)

6. Dragon-Finding Tips: In the American western states, look for dragons in areas of dormant volcanoes, especially near the northern edge of their range in Washington and Oregon. Obviously the dragons like the heat provided by these old craters. Placing a few jelly beans near these craters will sometimes lure a dragon out of its lair.

C. THE ORIENTAL FLIGHTLESS DRAGON

1. Appearance: Compared with the European and American species, longer, with shorter hind legs.

The forelegs are normal in both sexes. In addition, these dragons are distinctly crested, with antlerlike structures at the back of the head and with tendril-like whiskers near the nostrils. Generally greenish in color. The Japanese race is even more snakelike than the others of this species; its toes have been reduced to only three claws.

2. Habitat: Almost always associated with water; rarely if ever lives near mountains or volcanoes. Deep lakes and slow rivers are favorite habitats.
3. Vocalizations: Produces a thunderlike sound occasionally, by uncertain means.
4. Seasonal activities: Primarily active from spring to fall. The very best time to see dragons in China is on the fifth day of June, when they are always active.
5. Footprints and Spoor: Because these creatures are in water much of the time, footprints are rarely seen. However, the Chinese race would produce footprints showing four or five claws, while Japanese dragons would have three-clawed prints.
6. Dragon-Finding Tips: Look for dragons during thunderstorms, especially over water, since they then sometimes rise into the sky on waterspouts.

II. Flying Dragons and Pterosaurs

A. THE COMMON FLYING DRAGON

1. Appearance: Easily identified by its large wings (sometimes up to 10 feet across) and its capacity for prolonged flight. The wing beat is very slow, about one beat per second, and the dragons like to glide or soar whenever possible. In general, they seem to be very conservative in appearance but are able to change colors quite dramatically. Flights of dragons are always in linear formation; however, except during migration, dragons prefer to fly alone.
2. Habitat: Mainly found in the relatively high mountains of Asia and western North America, from Alaska to Washington. Breeding occurs in the mountains of Japan and Korea and may extend to the Kamchatka Peninsula in Asia.
3. Vocalizations: Fairly noisy while migrating, especially in September and October. However, their vocalizations show little evidence of structural syntax or informational content.
4. Seasonal Activities: Most active during May and September migrations. During late May and early June their mating displays are most likely to be seen.

5. Footprints and Spoor: Few footprints are left, since the dragons prefer to fly. Sometimes confettilike materials can be found where they have been active. Flying dragons are somewhat omnivorous and seem to be attracted to outdoor barbeques, picnics, and other sources of abundant food.
6. Dragon-Finding Tips: Do not try to enter the Siberian breeding grounds without prior approval from the Soviet authorities. The species is evidently periodically eruptive, and becomes more abundant every four years. The next major period of abundance will be in 1984.

B. PTEROSAUR

1. Appearance: Generally smaller than the flying dragon, with more sharply pointed wings. The pterosaur is essentially tailless and has several claws at the "bend" of the wing, instead of only a single claw. In general, its structure is more primitive than that of the common flying dragon.
2. Habitat: The pterosaur apparently was once very widespread but is now believed to be extinct. Mammoth and mastodon bones have often been found associated with pterosaur remains, suggesting

that a coevolutionary relationship may have existed between them. Perhaps they fed on the remains of these dead or dying ancient elephants.

3. Vocalizations: Probably relatively noisy, especially males. The vocalizations are said to be more drawn out and "drawling" than in the common flying dragons.
4. Seasonal Activities: Evidently active throughout the year.
5. Footprints and Spoor: These creatures rarely walk very far, so they probably never leave footprints.
6. Special Comments: These reptiles have been believed extinct for a great many years; do be very careful before adding them to your life-list. However, some fairly convincing sightings have recently been made along the Potomac River, in eastern North America.

III. Lake Dragons

A. THE BRITISH LAKE DRAGON

1. Appearance: At least 30 feet long, possibly up to 50 feet. The color is dark elephant-gray, and the neck is long and undulating. The head is relatively small, not much larger than the width of

the neck, and lacks a crest. There are four legs, all flipperlike.

2. Habitat: Apparently limited to the British Isles, mainly Scottish lochs.
3. Vocalizations: Apparently voiceless.
4. Seasonal Activities: Most often seen in spring and fall, but has been observed during all seasons at Loch Ness.
5. Footprints and Spoor: Evidently almost never goes to shore, but is said occasionally to capture lambs and sheep grazing at the shoreline.
6. Dragon-Finding Tips: Evidently is not attracted to bait such as animal carcasses. Look for the animal's wake on the surface of the water. It typically swims at about 9 knots, with only the head and upper neck visible.
7. Special Comments: Be careful not to confuse apparent sightings with mirages or floating logs, as has been frequently done.

B. THE AMERICAN LAKE DRAGON

1. Appearance: About the same size as the British form but more greenish in color; possibly crested or "bearded."
2. Habitat: Lakes of western Canada and the U.S., also rarely in eastern lakes.

3. Vocalizations: No information, but apparently voiceless.
4. Seasonal Activities: Usually seen during summer months at the peak tourist season.
5. Footprints and Spoor: Apparently never leaves the water.
6. Dragon-Finding Tips: Look for these creatures in the following lakes, where they have been reported recently: Lake Iliamna, Alaska; Lake Folsom, California; Lake Payette, Idaho; Great Sandy Lake, Minnesota; Flathead Lake, Montana; Lake Walker and Alkali Lake, Nevada; Hollow Block Lake, Oregon; Bear Lake, Utah; Lake Champlain, New York/Vermont; and Lake Waubay, Wisconsin. In British Columbia, Lake Okanagan is the best place to look, but there have been several sightings elsewhere in that province as well as in other western Canadian provinces.

IV. Unicorns

A. KARKADANN

1. Appearance: Similar to an Arabian oryx, but with a single horn, curved in a double spiral. Believed to be extinct since the 1600s.
2. Habitat: Open, grassy country and semideserts.

3. Vocalizations: A hoarse bellow that carries a long distance.
4. Seasonal Activities: Active all year, usually near sources of water.
5. Footprints and Spoor: Like the other unicorns but larger.
6. Special Comments: Very dangerous to approach! Cooing like a ring dove might be a good idea.

B. THE EUROPEAN UNICORN

1. Appearance: Recognized at once by the single coiled horn, which is present from birth. Sometimes confused in the field with the chamois (*Rupicapra*) of the Italian Alps, and possibly with deer elsewhere in Europe. Unicorns are generally much more shaggy around the chin and lower legs than any of these animals.
2. Habitat: Remote and unspoiled woods, with scattered open glades and unpolluted waters.
3. Vocalizations: In spring, the mating call of the male, a bellow or wail, is sometimes heard.
4. Seasonal Activities: Active throughout the year, but extremely shy at all seasons. The only times that two unicorns (a "charm") may ever be seen

together is during the mating period in early fall, or during the summer, when females are leading their youngsters.

5. Footprints and Spoor: The footprints of a unicorn closely resemble those of a fallow deer (*Dama*). They are about 3 inches long and symmetrical. In deep snow the marks made by the hair of the feet may be visible and allow for separation from deer prints. When walking, the individual hoofprint pairs are about a foot apart, and the marks made by the two right hooves often overlap, as do those of the left hooves. When galloping, the hoofmarks of the hind feet are in front of those of the forefeet, and each group of four prints is about 6 feet apart. When bounding, the four hoofprints are clustered, and separate clusters of hoofmarks are about 10 to 15 feet apart. Droppings and browse marks of unicorns cannot be distinguished with certainty from those of deer.
6. Unicorn-Finding Tips: One should never go out looking for unicorns; their sightings must always be serendipitous. The sight of just one unicorn in a lifetime is considered a wondrous event.
7. Special Comments: Unicorns need a great deal

of solitude, so if you value their well-being and protection, you should never tell anybody else of a unicorn's whereabouts.

C. THE ORIENTAL UNICORN

1. Appearance: Similar to the European species, but darker above and more spotted on the back; the horn is blunt-tipped and undulating.
2. Habitat: Remote virgin woodlands of southwestern China. Now extinct in Japan, and possibly in China as well.
3. Vocalizations: The male produces a loud bell-like call, much more pleasant than that of the European species.
4. Seasonal Activities: Active throughout the year.
5. Footprints and Spoor: Similar to those described for the European species. Be careful not to confuse unicorn footprints with those of the sika deer (*Cervus nippon*), which are distinctly smaller and closer together. Unicorns never step on living plants, and this trait may also help the observer to distinguish among various kinds of footprints.
6. Unicorn-Finding Tips: A trip to China to try to see this species is not recommended. One can, however, go to look for the giant panda of the same area and hope to encounter a unicorn.

Additional Information for Dragon and Unicorn Watchers

So far, nobody has yet been able to authenticate the existence of all ten of these rare species for his life-list. Indeed, few have ever seen more than three of them, and the current record-holder has claimed no more than six. No more than two have ever been claimed by a single person in any one year; and honorary membership in the Five-in-a-lifetime Club is restricted to those International Creature Watcher Association members who have accumulated sightings of at least five species of dragons and unicorns on their life-lists.

Experts in the field of dragon and unicorn watching recommend using at least ten-power binoculars. In the case of seeking the larger dragons, wearing a lot of mosquito repellant is desirable, since it seems to mask the odor of humans. Inconspicuous clothing should be worn at all times. Tape recordings of the animal's own calls are apparently ineffective in luring either dragons or unicorns, although the sound of jingling coins has been known to attract flying dragons and might also work for pterosaurs, if any survive.

When trying to authenticate sightings for

consideration as a contender for the world record in dragon and unicorn spotting, it is recommended that photographic evidence be obtained whenever possible. (However, one should never harass unicorns in order to obtain a photograph, and revealing the exact location of any unicorn is not considered necessary for certification of a *bona fide* sighting.) Photographs of unicorn tracks, preferably with a tape measure or ruler included in the photo, are also regarded as useful evidence. When intensively studying or photographing the European fire-breathing dragon, one might consider wearing an asbestos suit and carrying a pocket fire-extinguisher.

Finally, dragon and unicorn lovers may want to consider joining SPODARC, the Society [for] Protection of Dragons and Related Creatures. This is an international organization, open to all humans and other intelligent beings, regardless of age, sex, race, religion, or citizenship; membership is free and for life. The only requirements are a belief in the sanctity of life and a willingness to accept the right of unconventional but harmless life forms to exist without persecution or exploitation. SPODARC is also devoted to the preservation of enough wild places on this earth to support indefinitely a viable population of unicorns and other wildlife. However, the organization is currently under CIA investigation as a possible subversive threat to the U.S., and thus the address of its headquarters cannot be revealed at this time.

I am a brother to dragons.

Job 30:25

GLOSSARY

***Abyrne Deor*:** Anglo-Saxon term for a unicorn.

Alicorn: Term for a unicorn's horn (from the Latin *alicorna*).

Apep: The serpent-dragon of Egypt, a nocturnal creature who is constantly at war with the sun god, Ra. Also spelled Aapep, Apophis.

Arena: The display ground of a dragon, which is typically on elevated land, often with the ground trampled in the form of a large circle (see roundeley).

Awe: Proper term for a peaceful assemblage of dragons. See, also, peril.

Basilisk: A snakelike reptile, having a crested head, and often shown with two small legs. Also called cockatrice.

Chac: A Mayan rain god, similar in appearance to the *makara*.

Charm: The proper term for the sighting of two unicorns simultaneously, one of the rarest sights in nature. Thus, a charm of unicorns.

***Chiao*:** A marsh-dwelling Chinese dragon that sometimes dens in the mountains; also "Kiau."

Cockatrice: The "king of serpents," believed to have hatched from the egg of a rooster, and resembling a rooster in having a crowned or crested head. Even looking at a cockatrice is sometimes fatal. See, also, basilisk.

Dajja: A unicorn mentioned in the *Physiologus*, a thirteenth-century bestiary.

Dominion: A geographic area inhabited by a single, unified dragon population.

Draco: The name of the dragon constellation, near the North Star.

Dragonling: A newly hatched dragon.

Dragoness: A female dragon with eggs or young.

Drake: An obsolete English term for a dragon; firedrakes are fire-breathing dragons.

Ea: An ancestral Babylonian water god, controlling both wind and water; one of the earliest dragon prototypes.

***Einhorn*:** A German unicorn.

Eltanin: The "eye" of the constellation Draco.

Fafnir: The dragon slain by Sigurd.

Fawn: A baby unicorn (sometimes also called a foal).

Fledgling: A newly fledged dragon.

***Fuku riu*:** The Japanese dragon of good luck.

Gargoyle (Gargouille): A dragon subdued by Saint Romain of Rouen, France.

Grendel: A monster slain by Beowulf, believed by some to have been a dragon.

***Hai riu*:** A Japanese winged dragon.

***Huracan*:** A West Indian flightless dragon.

Karkadann: A ferocious Arabian type of unicorn of antiquity; from the Sanskrit *kartājan*, meaning "lord of the desert."

***Ki-lin*:** The Chinese unicorn (the male is *ki*, the female *lin*).

***Kirin*:** The Japanese unicorn; also called *sin-you*.

Kraken: A deep-sea water monster, actually a giant squid.

Kukulcan: The sacred serpent of the Mayans, the equivalent of Quetzalcoatl of Mexico. The latter is usually shown covered with brightly colored feathers. The rain god, Chac, is a related creature but is usually depicted with a long elephantlike trunk.

Ladon: A primordial dragon that guarded Hera's tree of golden apples and was slain by Hercules. Ladon was later awarded a place in the northern sky, as the constellation Draco.

Ley: The route traversed by dragons between their

weyrs and their display grounds; usually a fairly straight line connecting a series of hills, mountains, caves, and display areas. In China, these dragon paths are called *lung-mei*.

***Li*:** A hornless Chinese dragon, associated with the earth, rivers, and oceans.

***Lincorne*:** A French unicorn.

***Lindwurm*:** A German dragon.

***Liocorno*:** An Italian dragon.

***Lung*:** A general archaic Chinese term for a dragon. Specific types include *k'uei-lung*, the horned dragon, *lung-wang*, the dragon kings, and the *li-lung*, which control the earth and its waters.

***Makara*:** An Indian water dragon, usually depicted with the head of a crocodile or elephant and with the tail of a fish.

Midgard: A primeval serpent of Scandinavia, which was large enough to encircle the earth while holding its tail in its mouth, and which was hurled into the outer darkness by Odin.

***Monoceros*:** The name of the unicorn constellation (on the celestial equator between Orion and Hydra); also the generic name of unicorns.

***Mo-o-inanae*:** The Hawaiian mother of dragons.

***Naga*:** An Indian snakelike being, which sometimes

assumes the shape of a dragon. Various kinds of *nagas* drain rivers, control rainfall, protect hidden treasures, and guard the heavenly palace.

Nidhoggr: A primeval Norse dragon, who gnaws constantly at the universal tree, Yggdrasil.

Ogopogo: Local name for a lake dragon found in British Columbia.

Pendragon: The most influential dragon in an entire dominion.

Peril: A term describing a small number (usually under five) of dragons assembled defensively. Larger, more aggressive assemblages of dragons are properly called dreads.

Phalanx: A linear formation of flying dragons, usually in the form of a "V."

Python: A famous dragon of antiquity, killed by Apollo.

***Riong*:** A Korean dragon.

Roundeley: The circular display grounds of dragons (see arena).

Senate: A peaceful periodic assemblage of dragons.

Set: An evil god of darkness in Egyptian lore; the prototype of a serpentlike Satan in later Judeo-Christian tradition. Also spelled Seth.

***Sin-you*:** See *kirin*.

Smaug: A dragon in the Tolkien sagas (*The Hobbit*).

***Tatsu*:** A Japanese dragon type; the equivalent of the Chinese *lung*.

Thuban: A yellow star in the tail of the constellation Draco; the polestar of about four thousand years ago.

Tiamat (Timet): The primeval mother figure of Babylonia, and the female personification of chaos. Tiamat is the archetype of a destructive dragoness; in Babylonian mythology, she was eventually killed by Marduk.

***Tso'po*:** Tibetan name for *ki-lin*.

Typhon: A famous powerful dragon of Greek antiquity, who was eventually killed by Zeus. Typhon was probably derived from the Egyptian Apophis, or the Terrible One, who in turn was derived from the evil monster Set.

***Unicorni*:** Latin term for a unicorn.

***Unicornio*:** A Spanish unicorn.

Vrita: A Hindu serpent in constant strife with Indra, the god of light and goodness.

Weyr: A dragon's den or lair.

Wyrm: An Old English term, meaning any kind of serpent or dragon.

Wyvern (Wivern): Any dragonlike creature having

two wings and two legs, as opposed to the traditional type with four legs and two wings. From the Middle English, *wivere*, a viper, and sometimes also applied to two-legged snakes. See, also, basilisk.

Yang: The male element in the Chinese symbol of yin and yang; also symbolic of the earth, light, assertiveness, the number nine, etc.

Yin: The female element in the Chinese symbol of yin and yang; also symbolic of the sky, darkness, passivity, the number six, etc.

BIBLIOGRAPHY

Dragons

Allen, J. and J. Griffiths. *The Book of the Dragon.* Secaucus, N.J.: Chartwell Books, 1979.

de Visser, M.W. *The Dragon in China and Japan.* London: publisher unknown, 1913. Reprinted in 1969 by Akademie van Wetenschappen, Amsterdam.

Dickenson, P. *The Flight of Dragons.* New York: Harper & Row, 1979.

du Bose, H. C. *The Dragon, Image and Demon.* London: publisher unknown, 1886.

Elliot-Smith, G. *The Evolution of the Dragon.* Manchester: Manchester University Press, 1922.

Gould, C. *The Dragon.* London: Wildwood Press, 1977.

Hayes, L. *The Chinese Dragon.* Shanghai: Commercial Press of Shanghai, 1923.

Hogarth, P. and V. Cleary. *Dragons.* New York: Viking Press, 1979.

Huxley, F. *The Dragon: Nature of Spirit, Spirit of Nature.* London: Thames and Hudson, 1979.

Newman, P. et al. *The Hill of the Dragon.* Bath: Kingsmead Press: 1979.

Unicorns

Beer, R. R. *Unicorn: Myth and Reality*. New York: Mason/Charter, 1977.

Brown, R. *The Unicorn: A Mythological Investigation*. London: Longmans, Green & Co., 1881.

Freeman, M. B. *The Unicorn Tapestries*. New York: Metropolitan Museum of Art, 1976.

Hathaway, N. *The Unicorn*. New York: Viking Press, 1980.

Poltarnees, W., ed. *A Book of Unicorns*. La Jolla, Calif.: Star and Elephant Books, a division of Green Tiger Press, 1978.

Shepard, O. *The Lore of the Unicorn*. New York: Barnes & Noble, 1967. Reprinted in 1979 by Harper & Row, New York.

General

Baring-Gould, S. *Curious Myths of the Middle Ages*. London: Longmans, Green & Co., 1906. Reprinted in 1977 by Christian Classics, Westminster, Md.

Clark, A. *Beasts and Bawdy: A Book of Fabulous and Fantastical Beasts*. New York: Taplinger Publishing Co., 1975.

Costello, P. *The Magic Zoo: The Natural History of Fabulous Animals*. New York: St. Martin's Press, 1979.

Farson, D. and A. Hall. *Mysterious Monsters*. New York: Mayflower Books, 1975.

Frazer, J. C. *The Golden Bough*. London: Macmillan, 1911.

Gould, C. *Mythical Monsters*. London: W. H. Allen, 1886. Reprinted in 1969 by Gale Research, Detroit.

Leach, M., ed. *Funk and Wagnalls' Standard Dictionary of Folklore, Mythology and Legends*. New York: Funk & Wagnalls, 1972.

Ley, W. *The Lungfish, the Dodo, and the Unicorn*. New York: Viking Press, 1948.

Lum, P. B. *Fabulous Beasts*. London: Thames and Hudson, 1952.

Rowland, B. *Animals with Human Faces: A Guide to Animal Symbolism*. Knoxville: University of Tennessee Press, 1973.

Topsell, E. *The History of Four-Footed Beasts & Serpents*. 1658. Reprinted in 1967 by De Capo Press, New York, under the title of *The History of Four-Footed Beasts & Serpents & Insects*.

White, T. H. *The Book of Beasts*. New York: G. P. Putnam's Sons, 1954.

William, C. A. S. *Outlines of Chinese Symbols and Art Motives*. Rutland, Vt.: Charles E. Tuttle, 1974.